TRAIN FOR SOMETHING GREATER

An Athlete's Guide to Spiritual Fitness

W A D E   H O D G E S

For Heather

My Partner In All Things

Contents

Introduction: What If Jesus Did CrossFit?............................. 1

A Clear Definition Of Spiritual Fitness........................ 9

Measuring What Matters 21

Boredom Is The Enemy Of Improvement 31

Making Room For Others 41

We Suffer Together 49

Too Hard To Do Alone.. 55

The Great Humbling... 63

The Power Of A New Identity 71

You Are What You Eat 83

Rest Makes You Stronger 91

Stay Grateful.. 99

You Are Not Your Fran Time 107

Conclusion: For The Sake Of Others 117

Appendix One: Spiritual Fitness In 100 Words 123

Appendix Two: The Gospel Story 127

Appendix Three: A Brief Introduction
To Spiritual Formation 145

Appendix Four: A Parable For Church Leaders................. 151

Acknowledgements 155

About The Author 157

Introduction:

What If Jesus Did CrossFit?

Have nothing to do with godless myths and old wives' tales; rather, train yourself to be godly. For physical training is of some value, but godliness has value for all things, holding promise for both` the present life and the life to come.
                                                                -1 Timothy 4:7-8 (NIV)

It all started at a Starbucks in Tulsa, Oklahoma.

That's where I saw Mark almost every day. We sat across from each other in the comfy blue chairs in the corner of the store. We worked on our laptops, cracked jokes, and discussed the merits of Komodo Dragon Blend, our favorite dark roast coffee.

Once a week I'd ask him how much weight he had lost. Each week the number would change: 25, 27, 30 pounds lost. He was losing weight so fast it was dripping off of him. He would get up from his big blue chair and leave behind what looked like a puddle of melted butter. His transformation was impossible to ignore.

I had been yo-yo dieting for years and my weight hovered 20 to 35 pounds above my playing weight in high school. I was running, doing yoga, and lifting weights several times a week. I paid attention to what I ate, but still ate too much of whatever was on my plate. If I hadn't developed some moderately healthy eating habits, I would have easily been 50 pounds overweight.

Every time I complimented Mark on his weight loss, he would invite me to come work out with him. He was doing something called CrossFit. I had never heard of it. I kept telling him I would try it someday and then put him off for another week. But he persisted.

One day he emailed me a video of two people doing a CrossFit workout known as "Fran." It was unlike anything I'd ever seen. A ridiculously fit looking man and woman were blazing through multiple sets and reps of something called a "thruster" and swinging pull-ups. Just watching it made me tired.

Is this what Mark had been doing? No wonder he was melting before my eyes.

It looked incredibly difficult. It also looked a lot more interesting than spending 45 minutes on the elliptical machine at my gym. So in the summer of 2008 I did my first CrossFit workout. I'll tell you more about what happened in an upcoming chapter on humiliation.

The day after my first workout, Mark called to check on me. I missed his call because I was too sore to pick up the phone. I was hurting in places I didn't know I had.

A few days later I signed up for Elements, three classes that introduced me to all the basic movements used in CrossFit workouts. In each session I learned how to do movements with names I'd never heard before, much less attempted. They all felt awkward and unnatural. We closed each session with a short WOD[1] incorporating some of the movements I'd just learned. Each workout left me flat on my back in exhaustion and sore in a whole new set of undiscovered places.

Once I completed Elements I signed up for the cheapest three-days-a-week plan the gym offered. I jumped into my first real class on a Monday and got absolutely destroyed by a combination of pull-ups, push-ups, sit-ups, and squats. I had to use a giant rubber band to help me do the pull-ups. Even though I was in terrible shape, no one belittled me. Everyone treated me with respect and encouraged me to keep coming back for more.

A month later, I attended a free nutrition seminar hosted by my trainer. I wanted to lose weight, but I also wanted to improve my performance in the workouts. The best athletes at the gym took their nutrition more seriously than I did and I was interested in knowing what they were doing. During that 90 minute discussion, I was challenged to rethink much of what I had been taught about proper nutrition.

Just like the initial workouts, I found the first weeks of my new eating plan to be awkward and uncomfortable. But I stuck with it because of the results I saw other athletes getting while following the same plan. After a few weeks, I noticed I was feeling better throughout the day and my jeans were starting to loosen up a bit. Then the "melting butter" effect suddenly kicked in and my weight loss—along with my performance at the gym—accelerated.

---

1   CrossFit speak for "Workout of the Day." Not everyone who reads this will be familiar with CrossFit terminology. I'll do my best to define a few terms, but if I dropped a footnote every time I use CrossFit jargon, the footnotes would be longer than the book. By the way, this footnote isn't funny and not all of them will be, but I buried some of my best jokes in the footnotes, so keep checking them. You've been warned.

Three months later, while I was away on a business trip, my wife, Heather, scheduled a one-on-one training session with my trainer to check out CrossFit for herself. She had been skeptical at first. She didn't expect CrossFit to work any better or last any longer than any of the other fad diets and quick-fix programs I had tried in the past. She was also concerned for my safety, especially in the early days when I would come home drenched in sweat and too sore to help clean the kitchen. But my results were hard to argue with. I was losing fat I'd been carrying around since our honeymoon cruise 12 years earlier. In just over three months, I lost 30 pounds. My "before" and "after" pictures were stunning. Her skepticism ventured into the neighborhood of curiosity.

About this time, I decided that training three days a week wasn't enough. I wanted the freedom to come in and train as much as I wanted. When I upgraded to an unlimited membership, my trainer said, "So you're drinking the Kool-Aid!" I knew what he meant. While I didn't appreciate the allusion to being part of a cult, I couldn't deny that I was totally committed to CrossFit.

I still am. I haven't embraced it uncritically or with blind faith. I am a true believer because of the difference it has made in my life. I can't imagine a scenario that will keep me from doing CrossFit as long as I remain upright and potty-trained.

CrossFit has changed my life.

And my wife? It altered the trajectory of her life as well. She didn't just drink the Kool-Aid, she started swimming in it. At age 36, she changed careers and became a certified CrossFit trainer. She went from directing a preschool to teaching others how to do squats, pull-ups, and kettlebell swings.

Before moving to Dallas, we owned and operated a CrossFit gym in Austin, Texas for two years. I still love to get my WOD on and I have to force myself to take a day off. I get to tell my story and encourage others to try CrossFit almost every day.

I love CrossFit!

I also love Jesus.[2]

I've been a Christian all my life. I was raised going to church. I've been a minister for 16 years. I get to talk about Jesus in churches across the country.

When I'm speaking to churches, I usually meet Christians who happen to be CrossFitters. When I'm working out, I meet CrossFitters who happen to be Christians. In both instances, we talk about the difference CrossFit has made in our lives. We tell our transformation stories and show off our "before" and "after" photos.

We usually end up connecting our CrossFit experience to our Christian faith.

Sometimes it starts when they tell me how CrossFit has helped them overcome adversity and grow spiritually.

Sometimes I ask, "Do you ever think about what it would be like if church were more like CrossFit?"

Eventually they say something like, "You know, I wish I could get as excited about going to church as I am about doing

---

2   You don't have to be a Christian to get something from this book, but you do need to know that I'm writing from a Christian perspective. If you want to know more about why Jesus is so important to me, go read Appendix Two right now.

CrossFit." When I agree, they say, "It's a shame isn't it?" This leads to an awkward, guilty silence.

This silence bothers me, because I love CrossFit, but I love Jesus more.

So why is it that I've introduced more people to CrossFit in the last three years than I've introduced to Jesus? And why do so many of us find it easier to invite our friends to come with us to CrossFit than to invite them to church?[3]

Maybe it's because CrossFit has become a kind of church for us. The CrossFit community provides the connection, encouragement, and accountability we need to make and maintain huge life changes. We are accepted as we are and simultaneously challenged to get better everyday. We celebrate each other's victories every step of the way.

Or maybe it's because the improvements we're seeing in our physical fitness are outpacing our growth in the area of spiritual fitness.

CrossFit has taught us how to train our bodies for maximum impact. The gains are steady and our effort is rewarded with faster times, heavier max lifts, and better fitting clothes. CrossFit has made it easier[4] for us to pursue physical fitness by giving us a workable, maintainable plan built upon time-tested and reproducible principles that facilitate transformation in a variety of out of shape athletes with remarkable predictability.

---

3   To be fair to myself, most of the people I've led to CrossFit are out of shape Christians within my church network who needed CrossFit like crooks need Christ.

4   In this context, "easier" means "leaves you writhing on the on floor while begging your Higher Power to make the pain stop for the first 30 seconds after the workout is over."

Which means we're more likely to spend our time and energy training ourselves physically than spiritually.

Which brings up a couple of questions:

What if we pursued spiritual fitness with the same tenacity and intensity with which we pursue physical fitness?

What if we took CrossFit principles and insights and applied them to training for spiritual fitness?

That's what this book is about.

We love CrossFit and we love Jesus. Let's introduce them to each other and see what happens.

3-2-1 Go!

A Clear Definition
of Spiritual Fitness

Do you not know that in a race all the runners run, but only one gets the prize? Run in such a way as to get the prize. Everyone who competes in the games goes into strict training. They do it to get a crown that will not last; but we do it to get a crown that will last forever.

-1 Corinthians 9:24-25 (NIV)

The Goal Of Physical Fitness

One Sunday morning, my nine-year-old son and I were sitting in the large auditorium of a church building where I was about to speak. As he looked up at the impressive architecture he asked, "What would you do if all of this stuff starting falling down on us?"

While making a mental note to pay closer attention to the number of disaster movies he watches on TV, I said, "Probably nothing. We'd be crushed."

He replied, "I thought the reason you did CrossFit was to be able to run fast in emergencies."

Somebody get that kid a gluten-free cookie. He gets it.

One of the slogans CrossFitters love to throw around—and we throw around slogans almost as much we throw around bumper plates—is:

> What do we train for?
> Tomorrow.
> What happens tomorrow?
> Exactly.

We started doing CrossFit for a variety of reasons. We wanted to lose weight, look or feel better, get stronger, or improve our 5k time. While CrossFit helps in each of these areas, all of these goals are secondary outcomes to CrossFit's ultimate goal: *General Physical Preparedness.*

This is a fancy way of saying that CrossFit gets us *ready for anything.*

CrossFit's definition of fitness includes being proficient in all 10 established skills of fitness:

- cardiovascular/respiratory endurance
- stamina
- strength
- flexibility
- power
- speed
- agility
- balance
- coordination
- accuracy

Whether it's running fast or picking up something heavy once or moving something light many times, CrossFit prepares us for a broad spectrum of physical challenges without emphasizing one domain of fitness over the others.

This is summed up by another favorite CrossFit slogan: *We specialize in not specializing.*

Nothing spotlights this perspective better than the CrossFit Games. They have become a living parable of the CrossFit community's fitness philosophy. Athletes train for events that aren't announced until the day before the competition begins. Sometimes they don't know what workouts they'll be doing until they step into the arena. To compete in the CrossFit Games is to sign up for the "unknown and unknowable." The winner of the games is the athlete who excels across a broad spectrum of events designed to measure performance across each of the 10 fitness skills. The winner lays claim to the title "The Fittest on Earth."

CrossFit's definition of fitness is also functional. The point of the workouts isn't the workouts themselves. Rather, each WOD is preparing us for real life challenges, like running out of a crumbling church building that has just been zapped by an alien laser beam.

One reason for CrossFit's success is that it gives its athletes a vision for everyday, functional fitness that translates into everyday applications.

Soldiers, police officers and firemen love CrossFit because they know that being ready for anything can save lives.

A soccer mom does CrossFit so that she's ready to sprint down her driveway and grab her toddler before he zips into the street.

A teacher loves the way CrossFit gives her confidence to jump between two students squaring off in the hallway.

11

A graduate student does CrossFit so that he's able to help his best friend move his fiancée's piano up three flights of stairs.[5]

It's gratifying to know that when I walk into the gym to take on a workout, I'm preparing for the unknown and unknowable. With each workout I complete, with each new complex barbell movement I master, with each new personal record (PR) I set, I leave the gym with greater confidence. I'm getting better, stronger, and faster.

I feel like I'm ready for anything.

At least I'm ready for a variety of physical challenges. There are some things for which CrossFit can't prepare me. There are stresses, strains, temptations and difficulties that require more of me than the ability to do 25 unbroken pull-ups or deadlift 400 pounds.

The Apostle Paul articulates this deeper need when he tells Timothy, "Train yourself to be godly. For physical training is of some value, but godliness has value for all things, holding promise for both the present life and the life to come."[6]

Paul was no stranger to the world of athletics. He lived in a Greco-Roman culture that celebrated athletic achievement almost as much as ours. He uses enough athletic imagery in his writings to make me wonder what his mile time was back in the day.

While recognizing the value of physical fitness, he reminds Timothy that there is something even more important and beneficial, something that is helpful not only in this life, but in the life to come.

---

5   Assuming he can't come up with a good excuse to be out of town the weekend his friend moves.
6   1 Timothy 4:7-8

Paul calls it godliness. Another word for it is Christ-likeness. We'll call it spiritual fitness.

The Goal Of Spiritual Fitness

The goal of CrossFit isn't to work out in a certain kind of gym (industrial park garage, no mirrors, no air conditioning, no whining). The goal is to become a certain kind of athlete: one capable of taking on a variety of challenges across multiple domains. CrossFit's programming is aimed at forming just such an athlete.

The goal of following Christ isn't to attend a certain kind of church (contemporary, relevant, fun for the kids, no suits, no ties, no long sermons). The goal is to become a certain kind of person: one capable of responding to the unknown and unknowable in a Christ-like way. Your spiritual fitness training program should be designed to help you become this kind of person.

But do you even know what such a person would look like?

I bet you have no problem buying into the idea that a big part of being a Christian is growing in Christ-likeness. This is an appealing goal to believers and skeptics alike. How many people do you know who aspire to be as unlike Christ as possible? Even those who have rejected Christianity as an organized religion still see Jesus as a role model for how to treat others.

So when you declare, "I want to be more like Jesus!" you should expect few objections and plenty of pats on the back. There are, however, a couple of problems with your goal.

The Problems With Christ-Likeness

First, it's too broad.

Is saying "I want to be more like Jesus" really any different than saying, "I want to be a better person"? Noble ambitions, both of them. But neither goal is concrete enough to motivate further action or to measure continued progress. More specificity is needed.

Most people who walk into a gym want to get in better shape. That's what they say when they sign the contract.[7] But what does this mean? What does "better shape" look like? Without a clear definition of fitness and an intentional program for getting there, it's doubtful they'll make any real progress toward such a broad and undefined goal.

Most Christians want to get in better spiritual shape (become more like Christ), but they don't know what spiritual fitness looks like. Nor do they have a program for pursuing it. Another name for this is "unintentional non-discipleship." Not only do we lack a clear vision of where we're headed, we also have no plan in place to get us there.

What we need, beyond the general goal of spiritual fitness (Christ-likeness), is a clear vision of what kind of people we hope to become by following Jesus. This vision need not be complex, just clear.

Let's go back to the 10 fitness skills. While 10 is about three too many to remember, each one can be measured with motivating clarity.

---

7   In January.

- Speed is how fast we can run.

- Endurance is how far we can run.

- Strength is how much we can lift.

- Flexibility is how far we can stretch.[8]

What if we define spiritual fitness in terms of imitating Christ across a broad spectrum of spiritual skills or capacities? One example would be to use Richard Foster's six spiritual traditions from his book, *Streams of Living Water*.

Spiritual fitness includes, but is not limited to, the following domains:

- Contemplative (A life of prayer)

- Holiness (A life of virtue)

- Charismatic (A life empowered by the Holy Spirit)

- Social Justice (A life of compassion for others)

- Evangelical (A life centered on the Word of God)

- Incarnational (A life that sees God at work in everything)

Jesus excelled in each of these areas. When we say we want to become more like Christ, we're saying:

We want to live a virtuous life, steeped in prayer, rooted in the Word of God, guided by the Holy Spirit, filled with compassion for others, and infused with an awareness of God's presence in and around us, so that we're ready for anything life throws at us.

---

8   I could only remember four.

This is what spiritual fitness looks like. This is the kind of person I want to become. What about you?

This kind of spiritual fitness isn't the result of mastering just one or two skills. Rather, it comes from developing capacities in all six. We all have our strengths and weaknesses, but being ready for anything means we can't afford to ignore any of these categories. We must incorporate a variety of training exercises across multiple spiritual domains.

Sounds familiar doesn't it?

Are You Trying Or Training?

The second problem with the goal of Christ-likeness is that it is usually something we *try* to be instead of an outcome for which we intentionally *train*.[9]

There is a huge difference between *trying* and *training*. You don't wake up one morning and *try* to run a marathon, at least not if you hope to finish it on the same day you started. If you want to run 26.2 miles, you must go into strict *training*.[10]

Trying to be like Christ, instead of intentionally *training* for Christ-likeness, leads to failure and disappointment.

When I'm frustrated with the way I'm living and I find myself falling into old habits or getting caught up in destructive thought, speech or behavioral patterns, it's usually because I'm trying to run a race for which I haven't been training. We have to go into strict training if we want to run the race well.

---

9   For more on this see Dallas Willard's *The Spirit of the Disciplines*.
10   And yes, that .2 of a mile matters. Just ask anyone who has ever completed a marathon. They'll mention the .2 every time because it's usually the hardest part.

We'll pay big money to watch a handful of special athletes do their thing. Their mastery of their sport is both amazing and inspiring. One thing they all say is that when they're on the field or court or golf course, they don't have to think about what they're doing. Rather, they let themselves get caught up in the moment and allow their training to take over.

What if we can imitate Christ in a similar way?

When we find ourselves in a difficult situation—we have a tough choice to make or a rough temptation to face or an opportunity to speak words of truth and grace to someone in trouble—and the pressure is on to make the right choice or do or say the right thing, we are able to respond in a Christ-like way. Not because we're trying, but because we've been training.

CrossFit didn't invent the fitness domains. It took much of what was already accepted in the fitness community and found more effective ways to train across them. In a similar way, we can take the classic, time-tested spiritual exercises and use what we've learned from CrossFit to develop more effective ways of training ourselves to become more like Christ.

Here are a few exercises from multiple domains with descriptions of how they train us for Christ-likeness:

> Prayer trains us to connect to the heart of God and listen for his voice. (Contemplative Domain)
>
> Fasting trains us to be able to say no to unhealthy physical and spiritual cravings. (Holiness Domain)
>
> Meditating in silence trains us to reflect on our lives and discern what God is trying to teach us. (Contemplative and Charismatic Domains)

Service trains us to put the needs of other people first. (Social Justice Domain)

Bible study trains us to see our lives as part of God's story. (Evangelical Domain)

Worship trains us to see God for who he is and to live in constant thanksgiving for what he has done for us. (Charismatic Domain)

Fellowship trains us in the art of forgiving and extending grace to people who drive us crazy. (Incarnational Domain)[11]

General Life Preparedness

Beyond the specific spiritual domains and accompanying exercises, there could be an even simpler and more functional description of spiritual fitness: **being ready for anything.**

The promise of the gospel isn't that life gets easier for those who follow Christ. It's that as we become more like Christ we are increasingly prepared to deal with the unpredictable challenges of life.

---

11   A quick clarification about calling these activities spiritual "exercises." CrossFit workouts are designed to prepare us for unknown tasks and challenges. CrossFitters also know there is inherent value in each workout. CrossFit is fun and leaves us with a sense of accomplishment when the workout is done. Even though CrossFit is about preparing for the future, it evokes tremendous joy in the present moment. CrossFit would be worth doing even if we weren't preparing for the unknown and unknowable. In the same way, each of the activities listed above are inherently valuable. It is a mistake to reduce activities like worship, prayer, and service to mere "exercises" that train us for something else. Worship is a celebration of who God is and what he has done for us. Prayer is the intimate act of communicating with our Creator. Service is reaching out and helping others in their time of need. All of these activities are worth doing in the present moment for their own sake. That they are also training us for something greater is an added bonus. The only joke in this footnote is that I said it would be "quick."

When we pursue spiritual fitness with all of our being, we are training for something greater than general physical preparedness. We're training for *general life preparedness*. We're building habits and character traits that prepare us for whatever comes next.

The ultimate test of our spiritual fitness isn't how many verses we've memorized or how often we pray or how much we fast. These are training exercises. The exercises prepare us for the unknown and unknowable moments in life when the quality of our faith is tested. Then, and only then, will we be able to gauge our spiritual fitness and just how ready we are for whatever challenges come our way.

Training for spiritual fitness is the only way to be truly *ready for anything*.

Ready for success.
Ready for failure.
Ready for love.
Ready for heartbreak.
Ready for leadership.
Ready for opposition.
Ready for service.
Ready for temptation.
Ready for life.
Ready for death.
Ready for life again.

I'm not that worried about what I'll do when a church building starts crumbling around me. I do want to be ready when life comes tumbling down on me. This is why it's essential to always be *training for something greater*.

Here are the questions that will shape our spiritual training regimen:

What kind of person do you hope to become over the next 5, 10, 20, or 40 years?

What exercises are you using to train yourself to become that kind of person?

Every Christ-follower should have answers to these questions.

What are yours?

Measuring What Matters

But the fruit of the Spirit is love, joy, peace, patience, kindness, goodness, faithfulness, gentleness and self-control. Against such things there is no law.

-Galatians 5:22-23 (NIV)

Have You Seen My Stretchy Pants?

Heather and I recently enjoyed a trip to Spain. We turned our dietary consciences off and ate everything we wanted to, taking full advantage of the exchange rate between American and European calories. We ate a year's worth of bread, rice, and chocolate in one week. Upon our return, I stepped onto the scale and was pleased to find I hadn't gained any weight on my vacation from healthy eating. How did I do it? Before I tell you, you may want to find a pen. You're going to want to take note of this next bit of secret wisdom.

Ready? Here it comes.

I didn't weigh myself before I left.

When I stepped onto the scale after my vacation a number appeared. It was just a number. It had no context because I didn't have a "before my vacation" number with which I could compare it. Had I weighed before, I wouldn't have such a happy story to tell, but I see no need to let the facts get in the way of a good story.

There are seasons when I have a hard time eating healthy foods. Most of the time I eat lean meats, lots of vegetables, a little bit of fruit, and a trace of processed carbs in the form of tortilla chips and gummy peaches. Every few months, my switch gets flipped and I get caught in a cycle of eating too many tortilla chips which makes me crave too many gummy peaches which leads to too many pancakes which makes me crave too many bowls of Blue Bell ice cream. I think I just put myself into insulin shock.

During these seasons of gastrointestinal debauchery, I avoid stepping on the scale to weigh myself. Why? Because I know if I do, I'll be jolted out of my carb coma and I'll end up eating nothing but grilled chicken and spinach salad for a week. The only way I can maintain my bad behavior is to avoid the scale, because while I excel in self-deception, the numbers don't lie.

I tell myself not to worry. I'm not getting fat. I can eat junk food without consequence. As long I remember to put on my stretchy pants, I can carry on this pleasant fiction for a few weeks. Eventually, I have to put on a pair of jeans for a formal occasion and there is no place to hide. Avoiding the scale hasn't kept me from getting fat; it has kept me from facing reality.

When I finally do step on the scale I'm confronted with two kinds of news. The bad news is I've gained more weight in two weeks than should be mathematically possible. The good news is that having faced reality, I know what I have to do to get back down to my ideal weight. From there I can go to work and start making progress toward my goal. Along the way I remember the old adage that "no food tastes as good as being lean feels" and I promise myself I'll never hop off the wagon again. But I keep my stretchy pants in my closet just in case.

The Numbers Don't Lie

One reason CrossFit works is because it makes it easy to define success and measure progress. When you start CrossFit, you step on a scale, get your body fat measured, and do a baseline workout to give you a starting point for future improvement.

The results of these tests are sobering. Many of us think more highly of ourselves than we should and we walk into the gym imagining we're just a few weeks away from being back in the best shape of our lives. After our first workout we leave astonished at just how out of shape we really are.

The numbers don't lie.

This beginning snapshot, our "before" picture, is essential to making our experience with CrossFit fun and successful. As we begin to workout, change our diet, and get into a groove, we keep a record of how much weight we lift, how many reps we do, and how long it takes us to complete each WOD. Each note we make in our workout journal is a seed for a future celebration.

One of the most inspiring events to witness in a CrossFit gym is when someone gets their fat pinched and learns he's lost 3% body fat in the past month.[12] Then he steps on the scale and sees that he's lost 10 pounds. Then he does the same workout he did a month earlier—the workout that left him sitting comatose in his car for an hour before he could drive home—and he improves his time by four minutes. He's getting stronger,

---

12   Actually, it's cool to hear about it. Fat pinching is a "look away" moment for sure.

faster, and leaner. He knows it's not a product of his imagination. It's all right there in his journal.

The numbers don't lie.

Measurement also keeps us from fooling ourselves into thinking we are improving when we're really not. We tell ourselves we're getting in better shape. We're convinced we don't have to change our diet to lose weight the way other people do. These self-deceptions are believable for only as long as we refuse to submit to measurement.

Many CrossFitters find themselves at a crossroads when they realize they're still lying to themselves about how clean their diet is or how hard they're working in the gym. At some point, they face the numbers and either change their approach or quit.

Because the numbers don't lie.

Which brings up an interesting set of questions:

> How do you know if you're becoming more spiritually fit?

> How are you currently measuring your growth as a Christ-follower?

> Or are you wearing a pair of spiritual stretchy pants?

Measuring Christ-Likeness (Without Getting Rhabdo)

As with physical fitness, it is easy to convince ourselves we're in better spiritual shape than we really are. It's also easy to confuse activity with achievement. Just because you go to the gym a couple of times a week doesn't mean you're getting in better shape. Just because you attend church a few times a month doesn't mean you're becoming more like Christ.

Wouldn't it be great if our progress toward Christ-likeness could be tracked and celebrated in ways similar to what happens in a CrossFit gym?

Who says we can't?

Before we get too excited about this prospect, let's acknowledge a major difficulty and a potential pitfall.

One of the biggest difficulties in comparing physical and spiritual fitness is that it is harder to find tangible measurements for spiritual fitness than for physical fitness. The numbers may not lie when measuring physical fitness, but is it even possible (or wise) to measure spiritual growth?

Just because it's difficult, doesn't mean it's impossible. Social scientists have gotten quite good at measuring virtues like love, joy, and contentment.

I'm more concerned about the potential pitfall, which is that measuring spiritual fitness can lead to legalism. Many Christians live in constant tension with legalism—our tendency to turn the spiritual life into a list of rules to be obeyed. All sorts of bad things happen when legalism enters a discussion about spirituality. Consider it a spiritual form of Rhabdo, only far more common than its physical counterpart.[13]

---

13   From Dr. Michael Ray's article in the January 2010 issue of the CrossFit Journal: Rhabdomyolysis is a medical condition that may arise when muscle tissue breaks down and the contents of muscle cells are released into the bloodstream. One molecule in particular, myoglobin, is toxic to the kidneys and can cause kidney failure and, in the most severe cases, death. Rhabdo has been seen after high-intensity exercise.

Legalism turns our attempts at measuring spiritual growth into a way of making us think we're earning God's favor or as a way to demonstrate our supremacy over our neighbors who don't keep the rules as well as we do. It produces arrogance in the rule-keepers and despair in the rule-breakers.

Legalism is potent and toxic and has done much harm throughout the history of Christianity, so we have to tread carefully when we talk about measuring spiritual growth.

The solution, however, isn't to shun measurement altogether. In breaking free from legalism, many Christians have gone to the opposite extreme and allowed spiritual growth to become a private, and therefore unaccountable, extra-curricular activity. Avoiding legalism shouldn't be confused with pursuing Christ-likeness.

Measuring spiritual growth can certainly put us in danger of becoming self-righteous. At the same time, refusing to measure anything puts us in danger of self-deception. It's too easy to keep putting on our stretchy pants and telling ourselves we're doing better than we really are.

Self-deception can also lead some of us to believe we're worse off than we really are. Without some way to measure our progress, we find it hard to believe that the gospel has the power to elevate us beyond our self-described worm-like state. How do you declare a victory over the forces of darkness warring against your soul if no one is keeping score?

Without measurement there is less accountability and fewer celebrations.

The Core Competencies Of A Christ-Follower

So what can we appropriately and safely measure as we grow in Christ-likeness? Let's use the fruit of the Spirit from Paul's letter to the Galatians as a starting point.[14]

We can measure growth in the areas of:

- Love
- Joy
- Peace
- Patience
- Kindness
- Goodness
- Faithfulness
- Gentleness
- Self-control

First, we have to develop a working definition of each term so we know what we're measuring. Let's use love as an example. Followers of Jesus grow in love: love for God, love for our neighbors, and love for our enemies. How can we measure something as soft and squishy as love? In the New Testament, love is not an abstract noun. It is a verb, an action word. Love is described in terms of specific behaviors, many of which are listed in passages like this one from 1st Corinthians:

> Love is patient, love is kind. It does not envy, it does not boast, it is not proud. It is not rude, it is not self-seeking, it is not easily angered, it keeps no record of wrongs. Love does not delight in evil but rejoices with the truth. It always protects, always trusts, always hopes, always perseveres.[15]

---

14   Galatians 5:22-23
15   1st Corinthians 13:4-7.

Second, we have to measure our progress. Every Christ-follower should be able to answer the question: What evidence is there that following Christ has increased my capacity to love? To get the most accurate assessment we'd want to get a few of our friends and family to answer a few questions about us as well. If you want to know how well I'm doing at loving my neighbor, don't ask me; ask my neighbor.

If we say we're growing in love, but can't produce any evidence to support our claim, then we're probably still wearing our stretchy pants. If we can show how we are better at loving now than we were a month, a year, or a decade ago, we've tapped into the magic of "before" and "after" pictures. Our progress not only motivates us to keep growing, but also inspires others to investigate whether following Jesus could make a similar difference in their lives.

Milestones Keep Us Moving

As important as measuring progress is for newcomers, it's even more important for CrossFit veterans. The same is true for those who have been following Jesus long enough to have lost the initial thrill of having him turn their lives upside down.

Consider Helen: She started CrossFit six months ago. Today she came into the gym to get weighed, pinched, measured, and photographed. The woman in her "after" picture is 50 pounds lighter, looks 10 years younger, and unlike in the "before" picture, smiling from ear to ear. She achieved all of her six month goals.

Now what?

Most CrossFitters are usually pursuing some kind of milestone. It can be doing an unassisted pull-up, running a six-minute mile, or deadlifting two-times body weight. Milestones are unique to the athlete's strengths, weaknesses, and aspirations.

To stay sharp and motivated, Helen will need to set new goals and begin to measure her progress in other areas. Future improvements will be smaller—a few pounds here, a few seconds there--but every milestone she reaches will continue to motivate and contribute to her ongoing transformation. She'll never run out of milestones to chase and weaknesses to work on.

Consider Hank: He begins studying the Bible because of the difference he has seen Jesus make in the lives of a few of his friends. Eventually, he starts following Christ, knowing he needs to make some serious changes in his life. After several months of prayer, Bible study, and regular church attendance, Hank is being transformed in dramatic and obvious ways. He no longer has violent nightmares. He's cussing less. He's started doing nice things for his cantankerous neighbor. He's even stopped watching reality TV. His wife notices a difference in his attitude. His buddies can tell that something has changed. A year later, the differences between his "before" and "after" photos are staggering, but his progress seems to be slowing down.

Now what?

Like Helen, he'll need to set some new goals and begin to measure his progress in other, less obvious, domains of spiritual fitness. Future improvements will be smaller and harder for his friends and family to notice. But every time he reaches a milestone, whether it be to memorize a section of scripture or to cut by half the time he spends in negative thought patterns, it will spur him on in his pursuit of Christ-likeness.

No matter how long we follow Christ, we'll always have blind spots, habitual sins, and weaknesses to work on. There's always another milestone to chase.

Unless we stop measuring our progress.

Then we can put on our stretchy pants and start telling ourselves we're doing better than we really are.

What spiritual milestone(s) are you chasing?

Boredom Is The Enemy
Of Improvement

On the first day of the week we came together to break bread. Paul spoke to the people and, because he intended to leave the next day, kept on talking until midnight. There were many lamps in the upstairs room where we were meeting. Seated in a window was a young man named Eutychus, who was sinking into a deep sleep as Paul talked on and on.

-Acts 20:7-9 (NIV)

CrossFit Is Never Boring

CrossFit has been described in a number of ways: hard, challenging, scary, intimidating, frustrating, humbling, and painful (in a hurt-so-good kind of way). One word rarely used in connection with CrossFit is boring. Newcomers are struck by how much fun they're having even as CrossFit is kicking (and shrinking) their butts.

I was recently telling someone how by mid-afternoon I start looking forward to finishing up my work and getting to the gym to tackle the WOD. He said, "I can't imagine looking forward to a workout. I have a hard time making myself go to the gym two or three times a week."

When I told him I had to force myself to take a day off to avoid over-training he lost his friendly tone and eyed me with suspicion.

I don't blame him. I remember the old routine all too well. I'd come in on Mondays, Wednesdays, and Fridays and imitate a hamster for 20 to 30 minutes on a treadmill and then do a 20 minute circuit on the weight machines. Every day it was the same movements, the same machines, and the same TV shows on the little screen in front of me.

While there is something to be said for having a routine, boredom is the enemy of improvement.

In a CrossFit gym, boredom is about as scarce as a box of Cocoa-Puffs. We rarely do the same workout twice in the same month, much less two days in a row. Each day brings a different workout with different movements and new challenges. One day we're running and squatting. The next day we're doing deadlifts and pull-ups. A few days later we're rowing, jumping on a box and swinging a kettlebell. The duration of each workout also varies. Some last less than five minutes. Others are exactly 20 minutes long. A few can take up to 45 minutes to finish.

Televisions have no place in a CrossFit gym either. We don't need to be distracted so we can get through the workout. The workouts are distraction enough. The varied movements in a CrossFit workout are physically challenging and mentally engaging. Many are technical enough that we have to pay attention to each part of the movement to do it correctly. CrossFit forces us to live in the present moment. Many times during a workout I forget about whatever problem or difficulty I was dwelling on when I walked into the gym. It takes all of my mental energy to focus on getting through the next rep and then moving on to the next movement.

You never know what you're going to get when you walk into a CrossFit gym. That's one reason CrossFitters keep coming back for more. Some like to walk into their box not knowing what workout they're going to do that day. While they could easily look online and find out, they enjoy the surprise. They show up ready for anything.

Another reason some CrossFitters don't peek at the workout online is because they know if the workout includes a movement that highlights a weakness, they'll be tempted to skip it. It's human nature to gravitate toward things we're good at and comfortable doing. CrossFit forces us to address our weaknesses so we can improve them. If we pick and choose our workouts based on our strengths or preferences, then we'll have huge fitness gaps which limit our ability to be ready for anything.

Spiritual Adaptation

In exercise science, there is a principle known as *adaptation*. It refers to how our bodies adapt to doing the same exercises over and over again until our results plateau.

For example, if I've never done push-ups before, when I start doing them I'm going to show a lot improvement very quickly. But if all I do are push-ups, my body will adapt to the movement, my improvement will stall, I'll get bored, become discouraged and probably quit.

The solution to overcoming adaptation isn't to stop doing push-ups and start doing something else, but to mix up the routine by adding new movements to my program. Adaptation is one reason it is so hard to stick with a fitness program that prescribes the same routine day after day after day.

Many Christian gatherings consist of a handful of predictable exercises like singing, preaching, scripture reading, prayer, and communion; all done in the same order week after week. There is nothing wrong with any of these activities. Nor is there anything wrong with developing rituals around them. We need rituals to keep us grounded. Starbucks nailed it with a recent holiday slogan: *Take comfort in rituals.*[16]

But if the worship gathering is our only form of spiritual training, then once helpful rituals become dull routines, which leads to adaptation and stagnation. The only way to keep our growth from stalling is to seek out new activities and environments that stretch our comfort zones. This means we have to get comfortable with being uncomfortable.

For example, I struggle in small group settings. For 14 years, I worked with churches where small groups were an important part of our growth strategy. I had to force myself to be a part of every group I joined. As an introvert, I'm almost never comfortable sitting in a circle with 10 other people talking about my thoughts and feelings. If there is whining and crying involved, it takes a shock collar to keep me in place.

---

16   CrossFit has its routines and rituals too. While every workout is different, most CrossFitters have a specific warm-up and cool-down routine they follow every day they train. Many athletes don't feel ready to workout if they don't get to do their usual warm-up. Likewise, if they don't go through their cool-down routine, their workout can lack a sense of closure. CrossFit has found a way to imbed constantly varied training into the comforting framework of daily rituals. It's a powerful combination.

I love, love, love the anonymity of large group gatherings. I can sit on the back row, sing when I want to sing, listen to the sermon, and then sneak out during the closing prayer without being noticed. If left up to me, this is what participation in church would look like. This would be fine if I were a skeptic exploring the Christian faith for the first time or making my way back into the faith after wandering away. But it is unacceptable for someone who has been following Christ as long as I have.

If I gravitated toward my preferences week after week, I'd stop growing. I might even get so bored that I'd eventually stop coming. I need to be a part of a small group environment. Not because I naturally enjoy it, but because it's good for me, it is uncomfortable, and it gives me the chance to improve my relational skills and trains me to put the needs of others before my own.

I usually dread going to a small group, but afterward I feel better. I'm emotionally drained, but also energized because I pushed through my comfort zone. Sort of like how I feel after I've worked on handstand push-ups or ring-dips at the gym. It's not fun to do, but it feels great to have done it.

If I keep participating in a small group, it will get easier as I get better at it. I might even get so comfortable in the small group setting that my spirit will adapt and I'll stop growing. When this happens, I'll have to mix up my spiritual training to keep improving.

Take a minute and evaluate your current spiritual training regimen.

Are you suffering from adaptation because you keep gravitating toward the same activities? How has relying on your natural strengths and personal preferences caused your growth to stagnate?

What new spiritual exercise(s) do you need to add to your training plan?

A Spiritual Hopper Deck

CrossFit's constantly varied programming provides plenty of opportunities to enjoy using our strengths, but it also insists we train our weaknesses. There is even a method for choosing a WOD that is guaranteed to keep our training fresh. It's called the Hopper Deck. It's a deck of cards with a different workout listed on each card. Shuffle the cards, pull one out of the deck, and that's the workout for the day.

No excuses. 3-2-1 Go!

What if we developed a constantly varied approach to spiritual training based upon the Hopper Deck model?

The idea would be to convene a small group of people who wanted to train for Christ-likeness and embraced the concept of constantly varied spiritual training. The facilitator would identify 20 possible exercises that could be done by the group in an hour or less.

Here are a few possibilities:

Memorize a portion of the Sermon on the Mount.

Sit in complete silence for 20 minutes.

Go out to the surrounding neighborhood and take prayer requests for 45 minutes.

Write a letter to God expressing your deepest pain to him.

Write a letter to someone you need to forgive.

Write 10 encouragement cards to people in your sphere of influence.

Read a chapter from the Bible and write as many questions as you can think of in 15 minutes. Then come together as a group and spend another 15 minutes coming up with even more questions.

Spend 45 minutes preparing care packages for the homeless. Then take the packages you prepared and give them away during the week.

Sit in a circle and ask each person to spend 10 minutes telling their spiritual story.

Compile a list of all the things for which you are thankful.

Get with a partner and practice having a difficult conversation with someone you need to challenge or confront.

The facilitator would take these ideas and put them in a box. After saying a prayer asking God to guide the experience, someone would draw one of the exercises out of the box and then the group would do it. The group must be prepared to do whatever comes out of the box. No excuses. If special supplies are needed, then the facilitator has to have them ready. The group will spend the prescribed time doing the exercise and then come back together for the last 15 minutes and process the experience.

If I were in such a group, I would love to spend 30 minutes reading the Bible and asking questions. If we drew the card that said we had to walk around the neighborhood and take prayer requests, I would not be excited. But I would do whatever came out of the hopper because I need to train my weaknesses.

The group would come back the next week and do it again. They would work through the cards, never repeating an exercise until they've gone through them all. Constantly varied. Sometimes hard. Sometimes easy. Never boring. After a couple of months of this kind of training, every group member should be stimulated to grow in areas they would have otherwise never explored or addressed. A few might even find new strengths they didn't know they had because their past church experience had consisted of participating in only a handful of the same activities over and over again.

This Is Not For Everyone

I know what you're thinking. Not everyone will want to train for spiritual fitness in this way. This is true. Not everyone wants to do CrossFit either. This is one way of pursuing physical and spiritual fitness. It may not be the best approach for everyone. I wouldn't recommend trying to force it on an entire church. Rather, I'd invite a few early-adopters to try it as an experiment. It might turn out to be a more demanding path than most of us are willing to travel, especially if we've come to expect everything in our church experience to be in the sweet spot of our comfort zones.

But some of us—more than we probably realize—are ready to step outside our comfort zones, because we've realized that staying within them is taking us nowhere. We're willing to explore a new way of spiritual training because we're weary of showing up week after week, spending hour after hour on a church treadmill, and seeing very few, if any, results.

CrossFitters like to say *get comfortable with being uncomfortable*. If we step out of our comfort zones and embrace a constantly varied training approach to spiritual fitness, we may discover this to be an accurate paraphrase of Jesus' call to "take up your cross and follow me."

Are you ready to change your results by changing the way you train?

Making Room For Others

Then Levi held a great banquet for Jesus at his house, and a large crowd of tax collectors and others were eating with them. But the Pharisees and the teachers of the law who belonged to their sect complained to his disciples, "Why do you eat and drink with tax collectors and sinners?" Jesus answered them, "It is not the healthy who need a doctor, but the sick. I have not come to call the righteous, but sinners to repentance."

-Luke 5:29-32 (NIV)

I Need To Get In Shape First

When I invite my friends to try CrossFit, they often say something like, "Sounds fun. I'd love to try it. But I need to get in shape first."

When they say this, it tells me two things. First, they've misunderstood the purpose of the program. We do CrossFit to get in shape and stay in shape. If only those who are already in shape did CrossFit, our gym would be almost empty. Second, it tells me they're worried about being accepted. They don't want to be judged by people who are in better shape than they are.

I've heard people say something similar when putting off going to church or being baptized.

"I want to come back to church, but I need to change some things first."

"I've been thinking about being baptized, but I'm not ready yet. I have a few bad habits to clean up first."

Again, when people say things like this it tells me they don't really understand the core message of the gospel. Christianity is not for people who are already in good spiritual shape. It's for people who want to get in better spiritual shape and then stay in shape. It also tells me they're worried about not being accepted as they are. They fear being rejected by God or church people or both. Their fear of rejection keeps them from taking the first step toward a changed life.

One of the reasons CrossFit has become a popular option for people of all fitness levels is that CrossFit gyms have found ways to overcome this initial hesitation shared by so many potential athletes.

One thing you'll notice at a CrossFit gym is people at various levels of fitness working out side-by-side. Imagine three people working out together. One looks like he's been carved from marble and has 6% body fat. He's cranking out push-ups faster than you can count them. Next to him is a middle-aged housewife who has been doing CrossFit for only a few weeks. She's doing push-ups from her knees, because that's the only way she can do them. Next to her is a pear-shaped gentleman who has already lost 25 pounds in two months. Because his body shape makes it hard for him to do a traditional push-up, he's doing them from his knees and only going about halfway down. His form isn't great, but he's doing the work.

All three are experiencing the joys and pains of CrossFit even though they're all in different places on the "in shape" spectrum. One hopes to compete in the CrossFit Games where the winner gets a substantial cash prize. One wants to lose 15 pounds before she goes on a cruise in eight weeks. One has been told that if he doesn't lose 100 pounds he's probably going to die an early death and never meet his grandchildren.

This kind of diversity is possible because every CrossFit workout is scalable, which means that anyone can do it, no matter what kind of shape he or she is in.

And it is almost impossible to describe just how out of shape some people are when they walk into a CrossFit gym. They've never played competitive sports, lifted weights, or run a mile for time. They lack the flexibility to squat properly, the strength to do a push-up, and the endurance to run 400 meters without walking. They're addicted to sugar, can't imagine a world without white bread, and the only green thing on their plate is Jell-O.

Because they can't stand to take another step on their current path, they show up at a CrossFit gym. Immediately they are surrounded by people who are thinner, stronger, and faster than they are. They are put through a series of tests and asked to perform a number of seemingly impossible tasks. They leave the gym humbled by their experience. They wake up the next morning sore all over.

Then they do the most amazing thing: *they come back for more.*

I'm not surprised that once people get hooked on CrossFit they can't stay away from the gym. What surprises me is that so many people come back the first few times before they've seen enough results to fall in love with it.

One of the reasons out of shape newbies come back those first few times is because they are accepted as they are. This is one of the most important factors behind the success of CrossFit. *The CrossFit community upholds rigorous standards of fitness while at the same time making it possible for anyone to participate.* Every movement is scalable. Every workout can be adapted to the athlete's fitness level. Everyone who wants to, gets to participate. We meet you where you are and go from there.

But it's more than just scalable movements and adjustable workouts. It's also the way veteran CrossFitters encourage newcomers. Anyone who has the guts to walk into the gym is given instant support. A few days ago, I saw one of the most advanced athletes in our gym walk over and encourage a newbie after watching her struggle through a workout. He said, "Good job. Way to stick with it. It gets better. You should have seen me when I first started."

The CrossFit community is built on acceptance, but acceptance is also accompanied by encouragement to seek out better ways to move, eat, sleep, and live. Part of accepting people where they are means we're willing to give them plenty of time to decide to make healthy changes. Yes, the majority of people who start CrossFit need to change what they eat and drink, how much they sleep, and what kind of shoes they wear when they run. A wise trainer doesn't dump all of this on them at once. First, they are accepted as they are. This means giving them time to get comfortable in their new environment, to learn a new language, and to overcome the initial shock of just how out of shape they really are.

Over time, as they become more integrated into the community, they begin to notice differences between themselves and the more experienced CrossFitters. They start asking questions about nutrition, proper footwear, and ways to improve their lifting technique. It's amazing how many radical changes they make over time because they have been accepted into a community that not only shows them a better way, but lets them find it at their own pace.

How Scalable Is The Gospel?

An attitude of acceptance and the willingness to scale each workout so that everyone can participate is one of the principles that makes CrossFit successful. How can Christians overcome similar fears "out of shape sinners" have about exploring what it means to follow Jesus?

Another way of asking the question: How do we scale the gospel so that everyone who wants to can participate?

An important clue is found in the way Jesus interacted with those he was hoping to influence. He was known as a "friend of sinners." In other words, normal, everyday, non-religious people felt comfortable around him. The same couldn't be said about their attitude toward the Pharisees and other religious leaders.[17]

One of the biggest differences between Jesus and the Pharisees was the way in which they called people to repent. "Repent" is a nice religious word that means to change course or turn around. The Pharisees' message to sinners went something like this: *If you will repent, we will accept you. Change how you live, what you eat, and how you dress and you can be one of us.* For the Pharisees, repentance was a prerequisite to being accepted.

---

17   See Luke 15:1-2.

Jesus took the opposite approach. *He accepted sinners regardless of their past mistakes or the present messiness of their lives* **before** *they repented.* One of the most controversial aspects of Jesus' ministry was the way he gladly ate with tax-collectors, sinners, and other outcasts the religious leaders had labeled as untouchable.

In the ancient world, to sit down and break bread with someone was to say, *I accept you into my group, family, or clan. I accept you as a friend.* When enemies sat down to eat together it meant they were making peace. When Jesus eats and drinks with sinners, he's telling everyone at his table that they are loved and accepted by God.

When asked why he is eating with (accepting) sinners, Jesus tells his critics that he's calling sinners to repent by first accepting them as they are. He demonstrated that the best way to help change someone's life wasn't to exclude them until they changed, but to include them so they could see a better way.

It's hard to get in shape if the trainer won't let you work out until you're in shape.

Acceptance wasn't an act of politically correct tolerance from Jesus. He believed that every person he ate with needed to make some changes in their lives to flourish as human beings. He accepted sinners, not because he believed they were just fine as they were, but because he believed they needed, and even wanted, to change. He also knew they would not or could not change if they were always excluded by the religious establishment. His message to out of shape sinners was not *clean up your life and you will be accepted by God.* It was *because you are loved and accepted by God, you have the power to change the way you live.*

Acceptance is what keeps newbies coming back for more until they get the hang of CrossFit. It's also what empowers sinners to follow Jesus long enough to have him turn their lives upside-down.

What are some ways you can communicate love and acceptance to those you hope will one day start following Christ?

We Suffer Together

We also glory in our sufferings, because we know that suffering produces perseverance; perseverance, character; and character, hope.

-Romans 5:3-4 (NIV)

A Beautiful Kind Of Community

When I first started doing CrossFit there was a tough, older woman in my class whom everyone called "Mom." It was an endearing title for this spunky lady who showed up every day to train with athletes half her age. I later learned where her nickname came from. She was the gym owner's mother. When he wrote her name on the whiteboard, he wrote "Mom." So that's what everyone else called her too.

One day I showed up for class and it was just Mom and me. The WOD was to do five one-minute burpee sprints--as many burpees as possible in a minute.[18] So Mom and I did burpees together. I did them as prescribed. She had to use a few props to assist her in safely performing them.

---

18   Burpee is a misnomer. They should be called Pukies. They will also be the featured exercise in Hell.

On the first round I took it easy, not wanting to use all my energy too early. When the minute was up, we called out our number of burpees so the trainer could write them on the board. I was shocked when I heard that Mom's number was higher than mine. Mom out burpeed me! I snapped to attention and turned on the energy and ground her into a fine powder over the next four rounds. When the workout was over I was tempted to tell her I used the first round as a warm-up, but she probably would have said that she used the last four rounds as a cool down.

Nobody messed with Mom.

I've seen CrossFit create a beautiful kind of community spanning the gaps created by age, race, and body type. We may all lift different weights, jump on boxes of different heights, and run at our own pace, but if we push ourselves to the limit, at the end of each WOD we all end up at the same place—flat on our backs. After our initial recovery, we form a circle to stretch and cool down. There are nods of affirmation, fist bumps and high fives, and once we regain the power of speech, the phrases "good job" and "nice work" make their way around the circle.

Over time, mutual respect develops as we watch each other struggle through particularly difficult workouts that isolate our weaknesses. We all find ourselves wanting to quit in the middle of a workout as we sputter along while everyone else is powering through the WOD. The CrossFit code says that we don't quit in the middle of a WOD unless we're injured or lose capacity in one or more of our five senses. This means we keep suffering through a workout while everyone else who has already finished cheers us on. It's both humbling and encouraging when the early finishers gather around and motivate us to keep going. When we finally finish, they have a deeper respect for us because we didn't quit, and we have a deeper appreciation for those who kept cheering. We know we wouldn't have finished without them.

Several years ago I had a neighbor who was a veteran of the Vietnam war. One evening we were chatting about his experiences and he said, "Over the past 30 years I've been in and out of VA hospitals for all kinds of mental stuff. I tell you, if you gave me a chance to go back to Vietnam and walk the jungle again with my buddies, I'd do it in a heartbeat. I miss being with those guys. I miss the camaraderie."

He is still haunted by memories of the war, but he longs to go back and endure the hell of combat if it means he can experience a deeper kind of community than is afforded by the superficial relationships of suburbia.

Anthropologists call this deeper kind of community *communitas*.[19] *Communitas* is forged when groups share difficult experiences and overcome adversity together. We see it when a sports team comes from behind in the fourth quarter to win a close game, or when a team of entrepreneurs overcomes obstacles to make their dream a reality, or when a family rallies around a loved one who has been diagnosed with cancer, or when a group of Christians is being persecuted for its faith. Without difficulty, there is no *communitas*.

Every day I see a diverse group of athletes come together in our box and engage in voluntary, shared suffering. The result is a surprisingly deep level of camaraderie. It's not combat or persecution or cancer or a start-up company. It's not even a championship game. It's a small slice of the day when people softened by the comfort of their suburban lifestyles shock their system with some good old fashioned physical and emotional pain.

---

19   For more on this *communitas*, see *The Forgotten Ways* by Alan Hirsch.

It's *communitas* CrossFit-style.

Knock Knock

One of the challenges facing Christians in North America is that we have limited opportunities to suffer for our faith. Our neighbors are more likely to ignore us than persecute us. The closest most of us come to shared suffering is when we endure a boring sermon from a long-winded preacher while sitting together on the same pew.

Throughout Christian history, and in parts of the world today, shared suffering has given Christ-followers the strength to persevere through physical, social, and financial persecution. One of the reasons many churches struggle to create a sense of community deeper than a pan of brownies at a potluck is that they're not reaping the benefits of suffering together.[20]

This is not a call to go out looking for trouble. It is an assertion that our faith will benefit from getting together with other Christ-followers and voluntarily doing things that make us uncomfortable.

What we need is a training exercise that will launch us into risky, uncomfortable, and uncertain environments. Sounds like a perfect job for door-knocking. That's right. I just suggested the long-practiced, much-despised practice of going door-to-door and bothering people in the name of Jesus. Not because I think it's a particularly good strategy for sharing our faith, but because it's a great way to strengthen the faith of those knocking on the door.

---

20   This reminds me of a little booklet I once heard about called *What the Church Needs is a Good Persecution*. I don't think it sold very well.

It has been suggested that this is the greatest benefit to young Mormons when they go on their year-long door-knocking missions.[21] As you can imagine, Mormon door-knockers experience a variety of responses. They're rejected, insulted, ridiculed, and peppered with difficult questions. Repeated exposure to these challenges helps them own their faith and become true believers. It also binds them together as a group.

Please don't get lost in this example. It's not about door-knocking. It's about how overcoming shared adversity creates *communitas*.

The stories Christians tell about their best church experiences usually include some kind of group adventure emerging from an attempt to do something difficult. It may have been starting a new church in the inner city, transporting medical supplies on the back of a *burro* into the jungles of Nicaragua, or smuggling Bibles behind the Iron Curtain. Their tales drip with descriptions of *communitas*, and rarely include how they grew closer to each other by showing up and sitting on the same pew together week after week.

Have you experienced *communitas* before? If so, what were the circumstances?

What other kinds of challenging activities (besides door-knocking) would help Christ-followers experience *communitas*?

---

21   Trust me, it has been suggested. I just can't remember who suggested it.

Too Hard To Do Alone

And let us consider how we may spur one another on toward love and good deeds. Let us not give up meeting together, as some are in the habit of doing, but let us encourage one another—and all the more as you see the Day approaching.
-Hebrews 10:24-25 (NIV)

When You Don't Want To Work Out

I walk into my CrossFit class with a sense of dread. I'm anxious. I'm not sure I want to be there. I don't really want to do the workout written on the board. As soon as I saw it online the night before I said, "Oh no, this is gonna be tough." It's multiple rounds of handstand push-ups, ring-dips, and standard push-ups; three of my weakest movements. I'll have to fight for every rep and it will take me twice as long to finish as most in my class. Plus I'm having a "low energy" day. I ate too many chips at lunch. Most items on my to-do list refused to get done. It's like I've been trying to run across a field of almond butter all day long.

It would be so easy to opt out of the workout, go home, and take a nap, or better yet, go swim a few laps in a big bowl of ice cream. I show up anyway, ready to train my weaknesses and defy my sluggishness. Why? One reason is because I know there will be a handful of other athletes training alongside me. Knowing I'm not going to suffer alone is enough to get me to show up on a day when I'd rather be almost anywhere else doing something less painful.

It turns out the workout is harder than I thought it would be and I feel slower and weaker than usual. Yet as I say goodbye to my classmates and leave the gym, I'm glad I came in and did it. I know that tomorrow I'll feel better and the workout will be more enjoyable. But today, when I almost didn't show up at all, it was my CrossFit community that gave me just enough motivation to do what needed to be done.

I occasionally have to train alone because of travel or a weird work schedule. I hate it. CrossFit is much less fun when done solo. My times are always slower. Several times I've violated the CrossFit code by quitting in the middle of a workout because I just couldn't summon the energy to finish. I'd never dream of doing such a thing when working out with other CrossFitters. For most of us, if CrossFit were something we had to do by ourselves at home, we would try it for a week or two and then store our equipment in the garage with the leftovers from all the other exercise programs we started in the past.

CrossFit is too hard to do alone.

Knock Knock (Part *Deux)*

In the previous chapter, I described the impact door-knocking has on the faith of the knocker. Should you decide to go door-knocking, here is a helpful tip: never go alone. There's safety in numbers for sure, but that's not the only reason why it's a good idea to take someone with you.

Many years ago, I was working with a small church in the Pacific Northwest. Our building was in the middle of a quiet neighborhood. We were struggling to reach out to our neighbors. It was my responsibility to lead the effort, but as an introvert I struggled in this area of church leadership. At a time when I was desperate for ideas, I heard a speaker give a talk in which he described a new way to do door-knocking. Instead of going door-to-door and inviting our neighbors to church or trying to give them some literature, he suggested we ask our neighbors how we can pray for them. Ring the doorbell, introduce yourself and say, "I'm going through the neighborhood taking prayer requests and I was wondering if you have anything you'd like me to pray about." So simple. As soon as he described it, I knew it was something I had to do.

Eventually.

I put it off for several months. There were few things I'd rather do less than knock on a stranger's door and strike up a conversation. I blamed Jesus for my reticence. He taught us to "Do to others as we'd like them to do to us." Since I hated it when people come knocking on my door trying to sell me something or tell me about their church, I contended the best way to obey Jesus was to abstain from knocking on strange doors.

No matter how hard I tried, I couldn't get the idea out of my head. Nor could I shake the notion that this was something God was pressing me to do. One Saturday morning I told myself that if I didn't go through the neighborhood asking for prayer requests, I was going to resign my position as pastor of the church. If I couldn't obey the prompting of God and lead the church in an effort to connect with our neighbors, I didn't deserve to keep my job.

So I spent a couple of hours going door-to-door introducing myself and asking for prayer requests. The response from the neighborhood was mixed. Some slammed the door in my face. Some told me they already had a church home, as if going to church precluded them from sharing a prayer request with a stranger. A few were fascinated by my approach. I collected a handful of prayer requests. One woman even showed up at our church the next day to worship with us.

It was an amazing experience. I was intentionally putting myself far outside my comfort zone. I was going public with my faith. I was living out my convictions and setting an example for my church. It was probably one of the best spiritual exercises I've ever done as a Christ-follower.

And I hated every minute of it. Even though the results were positive, it was an excruciating experience for my introverted self. So I never did it again.

Some activities, no matter how beneficial, are too hard to do alone.

Don't Look, I'm Struggling

I had a good reason for not inviting anyone to join me. I didn't want anyone else to see me struggling outside my comfort zone. I'm accustomed to having my physical weakness exposed at the gym, but I've found all kinds of ways to hide my spiritual and emotional weaknesses from others. If my spiritual community doesn't always rally around me and cheer me on when I'm struggling, it's usually because I've managed to keep my troubles private. Remarkable community doesn't come from seeing each other at our best; it comes from seeing each other at our worst and then encouraging each other to press on to something better.

Let's return to the Hopper Deck model of spiritual training. Every training exercise has the potential to make someone in the group uncomfortable. So uncomfortable that they would never dream of doing it more than once by themselves. But because they're training with others, they get caught up and carried along by the momentum of the group. I've had several CrossFitters come into the gym and say about a workout, "This is why I love CrossFit. I'd never do this workout by myself."

One reason many of us struggle to regularly practice the traditional spiritual exercises is because we try to do them alone. While many of the exercises are personal, they don't have to be done in private. Some are just difficult enough that they'll never become habits as long as we attempt them solo.

When church leaders encourage exercises like quiet time, Bible reading, prayer, meditation, and scripture memorization, most of us probably envision getting up early in the morning and doing these things all by ourselves. While there have been many Christians who have done this and benefited from the practice—just like there are some long-distance runners who love to go out and run 20 miles by themselves—most of us will find such training to be more sustainable if we do it with others. Running club anyone?

What if we organized spiritual training groups where we come together to practice the spiritual exercises we struggle to do in private?

Let's Pray Silently Together

I've long been attracted to the discipline of contemplative prayer. I would love to begin every day with 15 to 20 minutes of being absolutely quiet and still, doing nothing but enjoying the presence of God and making myself available to hear God's voice should he have anything he wishes to say to me. As much as I want to do this, and as much as I've benefited from it in the past, I've never been able to make it a habit. Contemplative prayer is hard for me. My mind wanders. I get fidgety. I can always find something "more productive" to do instead of sitting still and "wasting time" with God.

Why must contemplative prayer be something I have to do by myself? Several years ago, I experienced the power of communal contemplative prayer when I visited a monastery that engaged in several sessions of contemplative prayer throughout the day. When it came time to pray, the members of the community didn't scatter and find a quiet place to pray in private. They all gathered in the same room, sat in silence, and prayed for 20 minutes. I was right there doing it with them. For most people, 20 minutes of silent prayer is just as challenging as doing as doing 20 unbroken pull-ups. What I discovered was that an exercise I found almost impossible to do by myself, was quite doable when sitting in an absolutely quiet room with 20 others.

My experience as a pastor tells me that most Christians don't read or study the Bible by themselves. The only exposure they get to the Scriptures is when they attend Bible studies, small groups, or worship services. The same is true for prayer and meditation. For many Christians, these exercises are too challenging to be done alone. They must be practiced in community if they are to be done at all. Even fasting becomes more doable if we know that 10 others are fasting on the same day we are and that we're going to get together later in the day to break the fast and talk about our experiences.

Spiritual fitness is a personal endeavor. We're responsible for our progress as Christ-followers, but this doesn't mean we should train in private. In fact, training for Christ-likeness is too important to be attempted alone.

Who are your training partners?

The Great Humbling

Humble yourselves before the Lord, and he will lift you up.

-James 4:10 (NIV)

The View From The Floor

CrossFitters have much in common: language (WOD, AMRAP, Pukie), diet (Paleo-Zone-Primal), apparel (Lulu, Vibram, Inov-8), and philosophy (pain is weakness leaving the body). Before we started talking, eating, dressing, and thinking alike, we shared a common experience: we were all humbled by CrossFit.

Here's the story of my first CrossFit workout.

I was curious when I pulled into the parking lot of the industrial park where my friend Mark's box was located. If I hadn't been looking for it, I would have never noticed it. There was a small sign next to an open bay door. Inside, the wall was lined with old school workout equipment. No mirrors, TV's, or machines. Lots of barbells, kettlebells, and medicine balls. Mark introduced me to his trainer, Eric, and my curiosity morphed into butterflies.

It felt a lot like visiting a new church.

Eric asked me a few questions, had me sign a waiver of liability, and explained that CrossFit is "constantly varied, functional movements executed at high intensity."[22] I had no idea what any of this meant, but it sounded good to me. To begin, Eric put me through a short warm-up that was harder than anything I'd done since my college days. While I was catching my breath, he introduced me to a "baseline" workout designed to assess my fitness while also giving me a taste of CrossFit.

When he wrote it on the whiteboard, it seemed like an innocuous combination of movements. I was going to complete a 500 meter row, 40 squats, 30 sit-ups, 20 push-ups, and 10 jumping pull-ups. I thought it would be a cakewalk, especially since I was working out three or four times a week and already in pretty good shape. This delusional self-assessment was based on nothing concrete except that it had been several months since I had to buy a pair of bigger jeans.

Just before I started, Eric said, "A good CrossFitter can do this in less than five minutes, but it will probably take you eight or nine minutes to finish it."

I grew up in competitive athletic environments. I was an over-achieving basketball player in high school. I knew a challenge when I heard one. I decided I would do the workout in six or seven minutes and then let Eric apologize for underestimating me.

He said, "3-2-1 Go!" and I started rowing, squatting, sitting, and pushing. I never got to the pulling part. When I finished my 20 push-ups, I stood up and walked over to the pull-up bar. I was seven minutes in and only had 10 jumping pull-ups left. I grabbed the bar and tried to collect myself so I could jump/pull my chin over the bar.

---

22   Translation: There is a good chance you're about to throw up the protein shake you foolishly drank before coming here.

What happened instead was that in my peripheral vision I saw darkness creeping up on me. Just before it pounced, I decided it was better to go down on my own rather than fall like a tree hacked to death by a lumberjack. The good news is that I didn't faint. That would have been embarrassing. Instead, I spent the next 10 minutes flat on my back, unable to roll over and stand up. Other athletes had to step over me as they went about their training.

I was delirious and kept asking Eric to call 1-9-1 as he hovered over me. He offered me water and kept asking if I was okay. When it seemed likely that my family wouldn't be testing the validity of the waiver he had me sign, he leaned in and said, "Welcome to CrossFit."

I call it *The Great Humbling.*

Rather than see my humiliation as something to be ashamed of, I now view it as one of the most important moments in my life. As I drove away from the gym and tried to remember where I lived, I was sure of three things: 1) I was going to be sore in the morning, 2) I was in worse shape than I thought, 3) I was going to submit to Eric and this CrossFit methodology that had devastated me in less than 10 minutes.

My great humbling busted open a door, barred shut by my self-deluded ego, to an even greater transformation. I lost over 30 pounds, weaned myself off of anti-depressants, and rediscovered a love for competition that had lain dormant in me for over a decade.

Almost every CrossFitter I know has a "great humbling" story to tell. CrossFit shows no respect for our fitness background. Bodybuilders, personal trainers, triathletes, former All-Americans, out of shape has-beens, self-deceived never-weres; it doesn't matter. We all end up in the same place: flat on our backs and begging everyone within earshot to make the pain stop.

First comes humiliation, then transformation.[23]

This is also the necessary order of things in the realm of spiritual fitness.

From Humiliation To Transformation

All the great spiritual traditions agree on this point: transformation, rebirth, enlightenment, salvation or whatever else you'd like to call it begins with a moment of insight in which we become acutely aware of our brokenness. In the language of the 12-step movement, we realize that "our life has become unmanageable and we lack the resources within ourselves to make things right." It's the moment when we finally understand that we're not as strong, well-off, or capable as we thought we were. It's the great humbling.

In the book of Daniel, there's a story about a great king who experiences a great humbling.[24] Here's the short version.

Nebuchadnezzar surveys his kingdom and says, "Look how great I am!"

God says, "Not so fast big guy."

Nebuchadnezzar immediately loses his mind, his dignity, and his power. Madness drives him from his palace and into the

---

23   My wife doesn't like the term "humiliation" in this chapter because of its negative connotations. I understand her concern. For many, humiliation is synonymous with shame. This is not the way I'm using it here. In this context, humiliation refers to the act of being humbled, which in my experience, leads to a positive outcome. Plus, I like the way humiliation and transformation almost rhyme.
24   Daniel 4:28-37

wild where he lives among the animals, crawls around on all fours, and eats grass. The original primal lifestyle.

Nebuchadnezzar thinks he's a god, so God turns him into a beast to teach him how to be human. His sanity isn't restored until he "looks up" and acknowledges his rightful place in the world. He's not a god, nor is he an animal. He belongs somewhere in between.

The story ends with Nebuchadnezzar praising God and saying, "And those who walk in pride he is able to humble."

First humiliation, then transformation.

When Jesus says, "Whoever exalts himself will be humbled and whoever humbles himself will be exalted," he calls us to choose humility, instead of setting ourselves up for a fall by thinking we're greater than we really are.

Very few of us accept his invitation to proactively humble ourselves. Those who do, can't go around bragging about it.

Unfortunately, most of us don't start paying attention until the great humbling is forced upon us. It can come in the form of an extended period of unemployment, a failed business venture followed by bankruptcy, the cruel dashing of a lifelong dream, a crumbling marriage, a tragic loss, or an unexpected diagnosis.

In an instant, we can go from standing tall, thinking we're in control of our destiny, to lying flat on the floor wondering what just hit us, and knowing we'll never stand up again without some help.

In that moment of broken, helpless, humiliating pain, we are on the verge of a great transformation. But only if we will "look up." When we look up we're putting our trust in something bigger than ourselves, submitting to a God who can teach us how to be truly human.

We don't find God by climbing to the pinnacle of our lives and looking down. The door to spiritual transformation is not found at the top of a staircase. It's found at the bottom. We find God when we descend to a place from which we can only look up and humbly ask for help.

First humiliation, then transformation.

We embrace this principle in the realm of physical fitness. We gladly tell our CrossFit humiliation-to-transformation stories. Yet many of us struggle to accept this same principle when pursuing spiritual fitness. Why?

Perhaps we've experienced more acceptance from our CrossFit community than we have from any of the spiritual communities we've been a part of in the past.

When you experienced the great humbling in CrossFit and were flat on the floor, no one stood over you and shamed you for being out of shape. What you got instead was a grim nod of recognition from every one of us, because we have all had the same experience. In your moment of humiliation, we came over and encouraged you, got you some water, picked you up, carried you to your car, programmed your address into the GPS, and told you to come back the next day so you could take the next step toward transformation.

Some of us have experienced exactly the opposite from our spiritual communities. At our most vulnerable, broken moments, we've been shamed, excluded, and made to feel worthless because we didn't measure up. Our humbling was magnified into something even worse than it already was.

It's not that we don't realize we're spiritually broken and in need of help. We're just scared to admit it because we're not sure we'll be supported and accepted if we do. We're afraid that when others find out just how messed up we really are, we'll be abandoned on the floor where we fell.

It doesn't have to be this way. We've seen the physical transformation that can occur when the CrossFit community helps us up after our great humbling in the gym. Imagine the spiritual transformation that can occur if we do the same for each other when life knocks us down.

What are some ways you can do a better job of helping your friends get up off the floor after their great humbling?

The Power Of A New Identity

So from now on we regard no one from a worldly point of view. Though we once regarded Christ in this way, we do so no longer. Therefore, if anyone is in Christ, he is a new creation; the old has gone, the new has come!

-2nd Corinthians 5: 16-17 (NIV)

We Are Athletes

Words matter, especially the words we use to describe ourselves. What we call ourselves, and what others call us, shapes our self-perception. That's why we called everyone who trained in our gym an "athlete."

A friend recently challenged the notion that everyone who does CrossFit should be called an athlete. He believed the label should be reserved for those who compete on a field, track, or court. "Athletes play sports," he said. "CrossFitters work out."

I told him that according to the dictionary an athlete is "a person who is trained or skilled in exercises, sports, or games requiring strength, agility, or stamina." He decided not to argue with either Merriam or Webster and conceded that CrossFitters can be considered athletes, in the broadest possible sense.

Sometimes it was our clients who resisted the label. They believed that because they never played a sport, they didn't measure up to the definition. No matter how much they protested, we refused to budge and kept emphasizing with our carefully chosen language that we had nothing but athletes training in our gym.

Even if participating in a sport were to be required to wear the label, CrossFit is the sport of fitness. The gym is our playing field and we're competing every time we write our results on the whiteboard.

An amazing thing happens when you repeatedly refer to people as athletes: they start to believe it. Before you know it, they're thinking, acting, eating, and training like athletes.

Convincing our clients that they really were athletes turned out to be more important than convincing them to cut their carbs or push past the pain in a tough workout. Their self-perception influenced their behavior more than all the great advice we gave them about leaning out and getting stronger. That moment when they finally accepted their new identity packed more power than magic on steroids.

We had one athlete rip her hands during a grueling pull-up workout. When she started CrossFit she was an out of shape soccer mom who wouldn't dream of doing anything that would leave her hands bloody and sore. Now she walked across the gym holding them up like a badge of honor.[25] When she walked into the gym office, one of our coaches, who was talking on the phone, quickly hung up to help her clean and treat her injured hands. This is how she described that moment on her Facebook status later that day:

---

25   We'd prefer she take care of her hands properly so her calluses wouldn't rip, but that ain't the point of this story.

"Brutal CrossFit workout tonight, but what a good feeling it gave me when I overheard my coach saying, 'Gotta get off the phone, I have an athlete here with ripped hands.' AN ATHLETE – yea, that's me!!!"

Here's how another one of our athletes puts it in her success story:

"I've learned that athletes come in all sorts of shapes, sizes, and abilities. I've learned that even though I was always picked last during recess and have never played on a single sports team, I can call myself an athlete, too."

That's the stuff long-term life change is made of.

This goes deeper than the short-term results of fad diets and quick-fix gimmicks. They may work for awhile, but the tips and tricks of external behavior modification eventually wear thin and most of us revert back to our old selves. There is no transformative power in temporary behavior modification.

The lasting life change CrossFitters enjoy flows from a new identity—a transformed self-perception.

That's why everyone who does CrossFit is an athlete, whether they believe it or not.

Preach.

Become Who You Were Born To Be

There's a great scene in *Return of the King* when Elrond presents Aragon with a big ole sword. The kind that is fit only for a King. He tells Aragon that it's time to "set aside the Ranger, and become who you were born to be." The time had come for his behavior to fall in line with his true identity.

Spiritual fitness is not about improving ourselves by changing our external behavior. This is nothing but religion and it doesn't work. It only leads to self-righteousness for those who play by the rules better than others and self-condemnation for those who can't keep up with the cool kids.

Spiritual fitness is the readiness to behave in a Christ-like way at a moment's notice, when the spotlight is on us and the angels are holding their breath. Virtuous behavior, when the stakes are high, doesn't come from *trying* to be like Christ. It's the result of *training* to be like Christ. A Christ-like response to an unexpected situation flows from habits ingrained in the heart over time. These habits grow out of and are held in place by our identity.

People who see themselves as athletes think, train, and act like athletes. But how must we see ourselves in order to think, train, and ultimately act like Christ? One obstacle to spiritual fitness is the difficulty in cultivating a powerful self-perception upon which habits can be built, and from which Christ-like behavior can flow.

Perhaps the only thing more difficult than convincing former couch potatoes that they are in fact athletes, is letting ourselves be convinced that as human beings, created in the image of God, we are loved and accepted by our Creator, just as we are, and not because of how we behave.

This is so hard for so many of us to believe. Just as past labels like "fat" and "out of shape" and "clumsy" get in the way of seeing ourselves as athletes, our true identity as human beings is hidden by the many negative spiritual labels stuck to us as we stagger through life.

Who do you believe you are? How have you been labeled in the past?

Are you *lost*?

A *sinner*?

An *outsider*?

A *stupid idiot*?

An *object of wrath worthy of hell*?

These labels may have been applied by well meaning, but insensitive and misguided, religious people who only know how to use negativity to manipulate the behavior of others. Or they may be self-generated. If others called me what I call myself throughout the day, I'd always have bloody knuckles. Regardless of the source, these negative labels rarely influence our behavior or shape our perspective for the better. They may scare or shame us into some temporary behavior modification, but they have no power to transform us into the likeness of Christ.

Long term transformation is rooted in a new identity. Physically, we are athletes.

Spiritually, we are . . .

Well, what exactly are we? What word(s) can we use to describe the way God sees us, words that will change our distorted self-perception and transform our behavior from the inside-out?

In *Mere Christianity*, C. S. Lewis uses the term "little christs." We are an extension of the hands and feet of Jesus on earth.

The word "Christian" can mean *little christ*.[26] Unfortunately, *Christian* has become a meaningless description in our culture. It communicates nothing of the radical shift in the identity of those who were first called *Christians*. *Little christ* is just off-center enough to jar us into considering the implications of wearing such a label.

In the New Testament, it's clear that Jesus expects his followers to carry on his work in the world. We are recipients of God's grace and blessings, but we are also instruments of grace and conduits of blessing to those around us.

How would beginning to think of ourselves as *little christs* change our posture in the world and transform our external behavior?

We Are Little Christs Now, Not Later

This new identity appeals to many of us, yet we struggle to embrace it. We hope to be transformed someday, at the resurrection, but it is hard for us to imagine ourselves ever playing the role of Jesus in this world. For example, consider the stories in the Gospels where Jesus interacts with someone and bestows a blessing in the form of healing, forgiveness, or wisdom. Usually, when we read these stories we see ourselves as those who are receiving the blessings. We're the ones in need of healing, forgiving, and teaching. Of course this is true. But as *little christs* we must also learn to read these stories from the perspective of Jesus. We are standing in his shoes and bringing a blessing to those with whom we interact.

---

26   I'm intentionally not capitalizing "christ" because I don't want to give anyone the impression that by saying we're *little christs*, equality with *The Christ* is within our grasp. He is King of Kings and Lord of Lords. We're not.

What difference would it make if as you went through your day you constantly thought of yourself as a *little christ*? What if every time you walked into a room you believed you were bringing the blessings of God with you? What if you saw every conversation as an opportunity to impart the wisdom of God to someone looking for truth by asking a probing question? What if you attempted to bring the healing power of God with you into every broken situation?

Maybe we resist seeing ourselves as *little christs* because it smacks of arrogance. The world doesn't need even one more religious zealot with a messiah complex. But Christ-likeness has a built in antidote to this disease. Jesus was the ultimate example of humility and self-sacrifice. If thinking you're a *little christ* makes you more arrogant, then you're not becoming more like Christ. The path to spiritual fitness leads to the emptying of self, the loss of ego. If identifying ourselves as *little christs* increases our arrogance, it's evidence we haven't been paying close enough attention to the one we're supposed to be imitating.

I Will Change Your Name

It takes time for many of us to accept this new identity and even longer to live into it. It may take some radical action from Jesus, or his followers, to open our eyes to the truth of it. One of his first disciples was a tax-collector named Levi (aka Matthew). Jesus picked him to be one of the first *little christs* to be sent out into the world. He entrusted the secrets of the kingdom of God to Matthew. After Jesus' death, resurrection, and ascension, Matthew continued Jesus' mission in the world, even writing down his version of the Jesus story (aka The Gospel of Matthew).

Before any of that could happen, Jesus had to break through Levi's distorted self-understanding and give him a new identity.

It started when Jesus invited Levi to follow him. It continued when Jesus invited himself to Levi's house for a party with Levi and his friends. Most of Levi's friends were tax-collectors and other "sinners." Tax-collectors and sinners were two categories of people the religious leaders of Jesus' day labeled and shunned as outcasts. So when Jesus enters Levi's house to eat with sinners, he's telling everyone in the house who had previously been rejected and excluded by the religious elite, that they were no longer outcasts. He was changing their identity.

This drove the religious leaders crazy.

One of Jesus' most famous parables was actually a response to the religious leaders who didn't approve of the kind of people he ate with (accepted). As he told the story of *The Prodigal Son*[27] there were two audiences listening with keen interest: the religious leaders who wanted an explanation for his behavior and the sinners who probably still had a hard time believing someone like Jesus was hanging out with them. In a world neatly divided into the "righteous" and the "sinners," the idea that the most righteous one of all spent most of his time with sinners was revolutionary.

What Are You Doing in That Tree?

In the Gospel of Luke, there's another story about how Jesus goes out of his way to give an outcast a new identity.[28] One day he's walking through the streets of Jericho and a crowd gathers to welcome him. In the crowd is a short tax-collector named Zacchaeus. He can't see over the crowd so he climbs a tree to get a look at Jesus. Jesus sees him in the tree and invites himself over to Zacchaeus's house for dinner.

---

27   Luke 15: 11-32
28   Luke 19:1-9

Inviting yourself into someone else's home wasn't a cool thing to do in the ancient world. Actually, it's not the smoothest move today. But there is always a purpose behind Jesus' strange behavior. A purpose that is revealed when the onlooking crowd grumbles about how Jesus is going to the house of a "sinner." There he goes again, hanging out with the wrong people. It's no accident that all of this happens in front of Zacchaeus's neighbors.

Once they get to Zacchaeus's house, we're not told how long they talk or what they talk about, but at some point during the meal, Zacchaeus stands up and pledges to give most of his money away and promises to stop using his position as a tax-collector to exploit others. Here is Jesus' ministry strategy condensed into a short story. Jesus accepts a sinner and the sinner responds to being accepted by changing his behavior.

Jesus answers Zacchaeus's pledge with a declaration, "Today salvation has come to this house, because this man, too, is a son of Abraham."[29]

"Son of Abraham" was a Jewish way of saying that Zacchaeus was a member of God's family. He is no longer to be identified as a "tax-collector," "sinner," or "religious outcast." Zacchaeus's pledge to change his life is the first step toward living into his new identity.

Jesus was already treating Zacchaeus like a son of Abraham before he called him one. There's a fun play on words in the story. Jesus tells Zacchaeus, "I must stay at your house today"[30] and then later says, "Today salvation has come to this house." The name "Jesus" means "the Lord saves." When Jesus invited himself over to Zacchaeus's house, "Salvation" is literally walking into the house to save another son of Abraham.

29   Luke 19:9
30   Luke 19:5

One detail in this story I always come back to is the image of Zacchaeus up in the tree, trying to see Jesus. What is he, one of the wealthiest men in town, doing in such an undignified position? Something must have been missing from his life. He must have been pretty desperate. Perhaps he was hoping Jesus could solve his biggest problem.

Remember when you first walked into a CrossFit gym? It may have felt like climbing a tree with the hope of catching a glimpse of someone who could help you. Perhaps you were fed up with the path you were on and were desperate to try something new. You probably came expecting to work a littler harder than usual and to learn a few tricks for tweaking your diet.

You never expected to be called an athlete as soon as you walked in the door. Nor did you expect to be doing all the previously unimaginable and seemingly impossible activities that only serious athletes dare to attempt. Yet now look at you: doing handstand push-ups against the wall, swinging on a set of gymnastic rings, and deadlifting twice your body weight. This is the power of a new identity.

When Zacchaeus climbed that tree so he could see Jesus, I bet he wasn't expecting that just a few hours later he'd be giving away most of his money and changing the way he did business.

That's the power of a new identity.

It makes us do all kinds of crazy things.

Who Are You Again?

It's not easy to embrace a new identity. If only Jesus would show up and do for us what he did for Levi and Zacchaeus. Perhaps he still can.

When speaking to groups, one of my favorite questions to ask is, "When God looks at you, what expression does he have on his face? Is he mad, sad, or glad? Do you make God frown, scowl, or smile?"

Unfortunately, many of us have a hard time imagining that God would ever smile while looking in our direction. This reveals our distorted self-perception. We think that when God sees us, all he sees is a sinner, a screw-up, or an idiot. If this is how we think God sees us, all the positive self-talk in the world isn't going to change the way we see ourselves.

Here's a guided imagery exercise that might help change your perspective.

Imagine that you're sitting at a table and eating with Jesus, just like Levi and Zacchaeus did. You're amazed that someone like Jesus would be willing to eat with someone like you. You're honored and also nervous, even a bit scared. At the beginning of the meal, Jesus plays the host and takes the bread and breaks it. As you reach to take a chunk from his hand, you feel the guilt of your last sin heavy on your fingertips. You're overwhelmed with the weight of all the ways you've disappointed those who are closest to you. When your eyes meet his, you see in them a knowledge of all you are and all you've ever done. It's all right there, in his eyes. He knows you like no other person ever has. As your shoulders sag and shame warms your face, Jesus smiles. He smiles AT YOU, as if you're the only person in the room. It's the warmest, truest, most authentic smile you've ever received, and it's coming from the face of God.

Can you see yourself sitting at the table with a smiling Jesus? Do you believe that you are loved and accepted by God? That

Christ sees in you a *little christ* capable of extending his love to others?

If not, that's okay. Just keep sitting at the table with Jesus, and with those who have fully embraced their identity as *little christs*, and eventually you will.

Once you do, you'll never be the same.

What is keeping you from becoming who you were born to be?

You Are What You Eat

Jesus said, "It is written: 'Man does not live on bread alone, but on every word that comes from the mouth of God.'"

-Matthew 4:4 (NIV)

The Secret To Physical Fitness

Newbies start CrossFit with all sorts of fun misconceptions.

"These super-fancy running shoes with springs in the heel will help with heavy back squats."

"Jumping higher makes double unders easier."

"A workout consisting of only 45 thrusters and 45 pull-ups can't be that hard, especially with a cute name like Fran."

"Since CrossFit workouts are so intense I really don't have to pay that much attention to what I eat."

This last one is what keeps most newbies from getting the most from their early CrossFit training. But if they listen to their coaches and pay attention to what more experienced CrossFitters are doing, they eventually discover the "secret" to taking their performance to the next level.

To reach your full potential as a CrossFitter, you have to pay attention to everything you put in your mouth.

"In plain language, base your diet on garden vegetables, especially greens, lean meats, nuts and seeds, little starch, and no sugar."[31]

One of the easiest ways to tell the difference between a newbie and veteran CrossFitter is the level of fanaticism with which they approach their nutrition. Some CrossFitters take the old adage "you are what you eat" to almost serial-killer levels of obsession.

We put our protein on a scale and measure it down to the last ounce. We count our almonds like a pharmacist counts pills when filling a prescription. We respond to white rice the way normal people gag when they see maggots at the bottom of a trash can. We stock our workout bag with a jump rope, tape, and—just in case of an emergency—a vacuum packed bag of all natural, organic, grass-fed, sun-dried, moonbeam marinated, elf-processed Dragon Jerky.[32]

I have no idea if this statistic is correct, mainly because I'm making it up, but my experience is that only 20% of leaning out can be attributed to CrossFit workouts. The rest comes from nutrition. In other words, CrossFit WODs will help you lose the first two pounds, but the next eight require you to *change the way you eat.*

When I started CrossFit I thought it was all about the workouts. I believed that if I showed up at the gym two or three times a week and did the necessary amount of sweating, swooning, and dry-heaving I would lose weight. After a couple of months, I had lost a few pounds, but other than a decreasing need to visit the abnormally green grassy area just outside the gym, I wasn't showing much improvement.

---

31   http://www.crossfit.com/cf-info/start-diet.html
32   Guaranteed to make you a fire-breather!

When I committed to weighing, measuring, and counting everything I put in my mouth, I started losing weight, my performance improved, and I enjoyed a greater sense of well-being throughout the day. After three months of steady CrossFit and a strict Zone diet I was back to wearing jeans I hadn't put on since the first Bush was president.

CrossFit is more than just a new and improved way of working out. It is a lifestyle that not only changes the way you eat, but also how you think about food.

If you really want to know how seriously a person takes his physical training, don't look at how many times a week he goes to the gym or how much money he spends on his workout gear or how often he tweets about how hard his workout was; instead pay attention to what he eats and how his food choices impact his relationships.

Once you've drunk the CrossFit Kool-Aid—an ironic metaphor for a community that considers sugar-laden drinks to be poisonous—you will never look at food the same way again. You'll soon find yourself disturbed by the junk your non-CrossFitting friends eat, and you'll start judging them, even though a few months ago you would have gladly joined them for a trip to the all-you-can-eat doughnut buffet. Your non-CrossFitting friends will find your new dietary restrictions to be amusing at first, then odd, and finally, downright inconvenient.

This can be a source of great tension between you and your friends. Relationships have been lost because of how seriously

CrossFitters take their nutrition. When you start choosing food over friends I'd say you're taking your training pretty seriously.[33]

---

33 Perhaps a bit too seriously, but we'll save that discussion for the chapter on idolatry.

Historically, one of the easiest ways for a group of people to differentiate itself from other groups is with a strict diet. This becomes an identity marker that builds cohesion within the group while distancing the group from outsiders.

In the Old Testament, when God sets Israel apart as his chosen vessel for blessing the world, one of the ways he reinforces this new identity is to give Israel a special diet. Not primarily for its nutritional benefits, but because it was vitally important for Israel to be distinct from its idol worshipping neighbors. They were to be holy. This God-given diet, which consisted of a list of "clean" and "unclean" foods, was one way to accomplish this goal.

The Jewish people demonstrated fidelity to God by refusing to eat unclean foods. One happy example of this is when Daniel and his companions refused to defile themselves while in exile by eating food from the Persian king's table. God blessed their choice and they prospered in a foreign land.

A more brutal example is the story about how seven brothers defy the tyrant Antiochus Epiphanes who invades Jerusalem and desecrates the temple by sacrificing a pig on the altar. When the king threatens the brothers with horrific torture if they do not eat pork, they all refuse and are slaughtered in front of their mother, who then follows her sons in death. At the time of Jesus, they were hailed as heroes because they would rather die than betray God by eating something "unclean." They took what they put into their mouths seriously.

By the way, how do CrossFitters describe their diet when it's dialed in? They say they're "eating clean." Interesting choice of words don't you think?

The Secret To Spiritual Fitness

In addition to being a way to set apart God's people from their neighbors, food is used throughout Scripture in symbolic ways to describe our relationship with God. A few examples:

- Adam and Eve rebelled against God in the Garden of Eden by eating forbidden food. They didn't take seriously enough what they put into their mouths and it destroyed their relationship with God.
- The words of God are equated with food. Jeremiah says, "When your words came, I ate them.[34] . ." "How sweet are your words to my taste, sweeter than honey to my mouth!" says the psalmist.[35]
- Isaiah describes forgiveness and restoration as an invitation to a feast, "Come, all you who are thirsty, come to the waters; and you who have no money, come, buy and eat! Come, buy wine and milk without money and without cost. Why spend money on what is not bread, and your labor on what does not satisfy? Listen, listen to me, and eat what is good, and your soul will delight in the richest of fare."[36] To return to God is to sit down at a great feast where the curse of Adam and Eve's rebellion is reversed.

Food also plays an integral role in Jesus' ministry:

- For his first miracle, Jesus turns water into wine. He refuses to turn stones into bread, but he will change water into wine. I like that.[37]

---

34   Jeremiah 15:16
35   Psalm 119:103
36   Isaiah 55:1-2
37   John 2: 1-11

- During a conversation with a woman at a well, he offers her living water that will quench her thirst once and for all. Later, when his disciples try to get him to eat some food, he tells them that his food is to do the will of God.[38]
- In his teaching, Jesus describes the Kingdom of God as a feast. "I say to you that many will come from the east and the west, and will take their places at the feast with Abraham, Isaac and Jacob in the kingdom of heaven."[39]
- Before he died, Jesus taps into the festive tradition of Israel and tells his disciples to celebrate their salvation and recall his sacrifice by eating a meal. For 2000 years, Jesus' disciples have remembered him with food.

In one of his most controversial teachings, Jesus uses food as a metaphor to reveal his identity and describe how his followers gain eternal life:

> I tell you the truth, unless you eat the flesh of the Son of Man and drink his blood, you have no life in you. Whoever eats my flesh and drinks my blood has eternal life, and I will raise him up at the last day. For my flesh is real food and my blood is real drink. Whoever eats my flesh and drinks my blood remains in me, and I in him. Just as the living Father sent me and I live because of the Father, so the one who feeds on me will live because of me. This is the bread that came down from heaven. Your forefathers ate manna and died, but he who feeds on this bread will live forever.[40]

If taken literally as an invitation to cannibalism, Jesus' original audience was justified in taking offense. When taken as an invitation to feast on the example and teachings of Jesus so as

---

38   John 4:1-34
39   Matthew 8:11
40   John 6:53-58

to be filled with his life-giving Spirit, it becomes the "secret" to spiritual fitness.

Going to church a couple of hours a week is helpful, but if not coupled with proper nutrition (feasting on Jesus) throughout the rest of the week, we can expect about the same results we get when we do CrossFit a few hours a week but pay absolutely no attention to our diet. We will realize no more than 20% (made up stat alert!) of our potential as Christ-followers.

You are what you eat.

What if as a Christ-follower you take what you put in your heart and mind as seriously as you take what you put in your mouth as a CrossFitter?

How would this change what you watch, read, and listen to when you're not "working out" at church?

Are you as fanatical about reading Scripture, praying, and listening for a word from God as you are about counting your carb blocks?

What's on your spiritual menu this week?

Rest Makes You Stronger

Thus the heavens and the earth were completed in all their vast array. By the seventh day God had finished the work he had been doing; so on the seventh day he rested from all his work. And God blessed the seventh day and made it holy, because on it he rested from all the work of creating that he had done.

-Genesis 2:1-3 (NIV)

Take A Break

A couple of years ago, we had an athlete in our gym who was drinking the CrossFit Kool-Aid with both hands. You could see it in his eyes. He was obsessed, maybe even addicted. CrossFit was rewarding his obsession with fantastic results. He was lean, fast, and strong. He was improving in every domain. I liked his chances of being a contender in our region for the CrossFit Games.

His only problem was that he refused to take a day off. He was in the gym every day pushing every system in his body to the limit. One day he mentioned he was fighting through a few minor, but nagging injuries. I warned him that if he didn't slow down and start taking a few days off from training, his body was eventually going to slam on the brakes and force him to take some time off.

I spoke from experience. When I first started CrossFit, I got hooked and found it almost impossible to take a rest day. I felt guilty if I didn't do some kind of workout every day, especially when I was in fat burning mode. I had this irrational fear that if I rested for even one day I was going to instantly gain back all the weight it had taken me three months to lose. I was also becoming addicted to the post-WOD high I'd feel driving home from the gym. When I did take a "day off" I would sneak in a few squats or push-ups or go for a long (two hour) run at home. I was a workout machine without an off switch.

Then I blew a fuse. I developed tendonitis in my elbow from doing too many pull-ups and trying to force a muscle-up before I was ready. My knee started to hurt every time I did box jumps. Then I strained my back attempting a heavy back squat.

I tried not to let my injuries derail my training, but training around a sore elbow, knee, and back proved to be impossible. One can only plank for so long. I would lay off of training only long enough to let my injuries "almost" heal. Then I'd be back in the gym a week too soon and re-injure myself.

It should be obvious from everything I've written how much I love CrossFit. It is hands down the most fun I've ever had working out. But I found a way to make CrossFit un-fun, and that is to over-train to the point of injury and then refuse to rest long enough to let the injuries heal. CrossFitting with chronic injuries is no *bueno*.

When I told my overtraining friend this, he politely listened, factored in that he is 10 years younger than I am, and kept on going. A couple of weeks later he blew a fuse while going heavy and was forced to take a couple of months off. He has yet to fully return to his previous state of awesomeness. He is a shadow of his former CrossFitting self.

What he once loved to the point of obsession just isn't that much fun anymore.

A Forced Day Of Rest

Several years ago, A. J. Jacobs embarked on an experiment of biblical proportions. He set out to obey every command in the Bible for one year. He compiled a list of over 700 commands, and did his best to obey every one. Afterward, he wrote a book about his experiences entitled *The Year of Living Biblically*. It was an instant bestseller.

While doing publicity for the book, he was asked if there were any commands he continued to observe after his experiment was over. He answered, "There's a lot about gratefulness in the Bible, and I would say I'm more thankful ... *and I love the Sabbath. There's something I really like about a forced day of rest.*"

Most followers of Jesus aren't sure what to do with the Sabbath. In the New Testament, we're never commanded to keep the Sabbath in an old school sort of way. It is the only one of the original 10 Commandments that isn't re-stated in the teachings of Jesus or the writings of his earliest followers. Many of us are happy to leave the Sabbath behind in the archaic pages of the Old Testament. "Whew! I'm glad we don't have to worry about that one anymore."

I understand why. Jacobs is right to call the Sabbath "a forced day of rest." In the Old Testament, the penalties for working on the Sabbath were harsh. Here's one example:

> Then the Lord said to Moses, "Say to the Israelites, 'You must observe my Sabbaths. This will be a sign between me and you for the generations to come, so you may know that I am the Lord, who makes you holy. ... For six days, work is

to be done, but the seventh day is a Sabbath of rest, holy to the Lord. Whoever does any work on the Sabbath day must be put to death.'"[41]

And you think your gym's 10 burpee penalty for dropping a kettlebell is over the top?

Why is such a punishment necessary? Simple really. Because people kept working on the Sabbath. They couldn't help themselves. They felt compelled to move a little dirt from here to there, or to scatter a few seeds behind their tent, or to pick a squash from the garden. They were addicted to productivity. They couldn't make themselves take a day off.

Why is the punishment so extreme? Because the Sabbath was a sign of Israel's relationship with God. If Israel refused to take the Sabbath seriously, then it meant they weren't taking their relationship with God seriously either. God saved Israel from slavery in Egypt and promised to take care of Israel by providing everything the people needed to survive in the wilderness and beyond. All Israel had to do was demonstrate their trust in God by keeping his commands, especially the one about keeping the Sabbath.

There is a stunning connection between Israel's unwillingness to observe the Sabbath and its penchant for worshipping idols.[42] Not trusting God enough to rest one day a week opens Israel up to chasing after false gods and developing all sorts of destructive obsessions.

When an Israelite worked on the Sabbath, it was a confession of distrust. A way of saying, "I'm not sure I trust God to take care of my family and me. I had better take care of myself."

---

41   Exodus 31:12-15
42   Ezekiel 20:12-24

This was the beginning of the end for ancient Israel.

Rest is a form of trust.

Trust The Sacred Rhythm

Why do CrossFitters over-train? Why do some of us find it almost impossible to take a day off, even when the official CrossFit.com prescription is three days of work followed by a day of rest? Because we don't trust the program. We don't trust the principle that *rest is also a form of working out.* We struggle to believe that it's on our days off, as our body is repairing itself, that we're making gains in strength and speed.

So we reject the wisdom of our coaches, more experienced athletes, and scientists. We scoff at the need for an off switch. It's only after our body forces the issue—too late in most cases—that we decide it might be a good idea to put our trust in a program designed by someone who knows more about achieving fitness than we do. What could have been a simple practice of taking every fourth day off, ends up being a month on the sidelines practicing the hook grip on a PVC pipe.

Three on, one off. Three on, one off. Three on, one off. This is the rhythm of elite fitness. But only if we trust the rhythm enough to actually take a day off.

Even though keeping the Sabbath is not a requirement for being a follower of Jesus, I challenge the wisdom of completely setting aside the Sabbath principle. It was, after all, part of the sacred rhythm established in the story of creation found at the beginning of the Bible.

Long before the Sabbath made God's top 10 list of commands, or emerged as the sign of God's special relationship with Israel, or came attached with a death penalty for all who ignored it; it was a day of rest enjoyed by the creator of the universe. This day of rest was so important to God that it was the first thing he blessed and set apart for holy purposes.

Dare we ignore the example of our Creator who established at creation a sacred rhythm, a holy cadence meant to dictate the pace of our work?

When we ask, "Do we HAVE to observe the Sabbath? Do we HAVE to take a day off?" like it's a heavy load that has to be carried up a steep mountain, we're missing the point. Jesus said, "The Sabbath was made for man, not man for the Sabbath."[43] The Sabbath was intended to be a blessing, not a burden. This is why A. J. Jacobs proclaimed, "I love the Sabbath!"

Six on, one off. Six on, one off. Six on, one off. This is the rhythm of a well-balanced life, lived in sync with our Creator.

If we trust God enough to actually take a day off.

Rest Is Hard Work

The lessons we learn in a CrossFit gym—the necessity of hard work, the importance of taking responsibility for our weaknesses, the value of hustling—all translate into other areas of our lives. These attributes allow us to make positive contributions to the world through the companies we build, projects we complete, tasks we accomplish, and households we manage. Six days a week they empower us to do the good work God has created us to do.

But without an off switch, these same attributes can turn our work into an idol. They give us the illusion of control, that

---

43   Mark 2:27

we're in charge of our destiny. They enhance our sense of self-importance by keeping us busy. They make us wildly productive, which can fuel our addiction to being needed or to pleasing others with our performance.

This is why rest is such hard work for so many people.

When we take a day off, we give up control of our little world and trust God to mind the store while we're away. Rest forces us to find our sense of worth in our relationship with God instead of our accomplishments. Rest keeps us from taking ourselves too seriously. Rest encourages us to stop trying to get from our work what only God can give. Our work is good, but it is not God. Rest saves us from idolatry.

We cannot be spiritually fit without rest. We cannot be ready for anything if we're on the verge of blowing a fuse.

Do you think you can you do it? Can you take a day off and rest?

The day doesn't really matter. Saturday or Sunday works best for most, but there's no need to be a legalist. The Sabbath was made to serve us. We were not made to serve the Sabbath.

Do you really think you can do it?

No work related email, texts, phone calls, or social media. Who are we kidding? Technology has blurred the lines between professional and personal time. You better lock your Crackberry or i(dol)Pad in the trunk and give the keys to those who crave your full attention.

Don't worry, the world will get along just fine without you. You're not as important as you think you are. God will hold things together while you do nothing. You might even find that after a day a rest you return to work with more energy and insight than you had before. What if rest makes you stronger? Why not try it and find out?

In the days of old, ignoring the Sabbath could get you killed. When we ignore the Sabbath principle today, we're still putting ourselves in peril, not because someone is going to catch us working and hit us upside the head with a rock, but because our chronic busyness and compulsive productivity is destroying us.

Don't practice the Sabbath principle to keep from getting killed; practice it as a way to stay fully alive.

What is keeping you from resting?

Stay Grateful

"My grace is sufficient for you, for my power is made perfect in weakness." Therefore I will boast all the more gladly about my weaknesses, so that Christ's power may rest on me. That is why, for Christ's sake, I delight in weaknesses, in insults, in hardships, in persecutions, in difficulties. For when I am weak, then I am strong.

-2 Corinthians 12:9-10 (NIV)

The Ugly Side Of CrossFit

One of the knocks against CrossFit is that many CrossFitters come across as arrogant to outsiders. Where are they getting this impression? I have no idea.

Wanna buy a T-shirt? Here are a few of the more popular options:

"CrossFit: Our Warm-up is Your Workout"

"The Girls at My Gym Can Beat Up the Guys at Yours"

"Your Gym Sucks"

These slogans do a great job articulating the judgmental attitude many CrossFitters display toward others who aren't working out as hard or eating as clean as they are. In addition to wearing the shirts, they make snide comments to their friends about how they're not really serious about fitness because they've yet to embrace the glory of CrossFit. Such arrogant exclusivity is one of the few negative side effects of the CrossFit Kool-Aid. This is both tragic and ironic.

It's tragic because arrogance is rarely attractive. Judging and insulting others who don't pursue fitness the same way we do is not the best way to invite others to join our community.

"Hey you carb-sucking fatso! Get your hand off the Twinkies and your butt off the elliptical and let us teach you the right way to workout."

"Okay. Sounds fun. Thanks for caring enough to insult me."

Sometimes I wonder how fast CrossFit would be growing if so many CrossFitters weren't such jerks about how CrossFit is the only way to pursue elite fitness.

CrossFit arrogance is ironic in that the average jerky Cross-Fitter didn't have a clue it even existed three years ago and can take zero credit for developing it into the world's greatest fitness program.

It wasn't that long ago when we were all on the treadmill of conventional fitness, doing long sessions of cardio while watching TV or moving through a circuit of weight machines while our iPods blasted a motivational playlist. We were congratulating ourselves for eating a high carb snack because it was low in fat or because we had taken a stand and started buying products made with real sugar instead of high-fructose corn syrup.

I'm not describing CrossFit arrogance as an innocent bystander. I'm a full-fledged participant. The first year I did CrossFit I maintained my membership at my globo gym because it was cheap and I enjoyed dropping in on an occasional yoga class. The deeper I got into CrossFit and the more I learned about proper standards of movement, the harder it was to walk through the free weight area on the way to the yoga room. I had to avert my eyes from the dude standing in the squat rack or else I'd lose control and scream, "You have no right to grunt like that if you're only going to go halfway down!"

When I see someone loading up a plate with pasta and chasing it down with a side of garlic bread I want to go over and grab him by the love handles and tell him the sluggish feeling coming his way in 30 minutes is his body's way of saying, "You're killing me with this crap!"

Never mind that five years ago you would have found me doing the same things, and much worse.

How quickly we forget that CrossFit comes with a built-in humiliator. It toys with our confidence while exposing our weaknesses. Every CrossFitter, no matter how accomplished, has one or two domains or movements that don't quite measure up to the rest. Just because you went into beast mode in yesterday's workout doesn't mean you won't be sitting in a corner with your head in your hands wondering why you even bothered to show up at the gym later today.

How can a program with a knack for reminding us just how far away we are from elite fitness breed so much arrogance and exclusivity in athletes who still can't overhead squat their bodyweight or do 21 unbroken handstand push-ups or do a strict muscle-up or _____ (insert your goat here)?

What gives me (or you) the right to display even a hint of arrogance to those outside of CrossFit community?

I didn't formulate the Paleo-Zone diet.[44] I didn't invent CrossFit. If it weren't for multiple invitations from a persistent (and humble) friend, I wouldn't have tried it. I was blessed to have a good gym with a great trainer nearby. I didn't deserve the opportunity to explore a new way of chasing fitness. I certainly haven't earned the right to be a jerk to those who have yet to try CrossFit or have decided it's not the best program for them.

My CrossFit experience has been a gift. Something for which I'm profoundly grateful. It's only when I lose touch with this deep sense of gratitude that my CrossFit arrogance goes on a rampage.

The Ugly Side Of Christianity

I'm particularly sensitive to this kind of arrogance in myself and other CrossFitters because I recognize a similar arrogance in the Christian community. One of the primary stereotypes non-Christians point to when explaining why contemporary Christianity lacks credibility in their eyes is the arrogant, judgmental attitudes of the Christians they know personally and see on TV.

I know these stereotypes aren't just caricatures from people with an anti-Christian agenda, because I've done my fair share of contributing to their perceptions. I've worked with churches where the majority of members believe that anyone who isn't a part of their community or doesn't believe exactly what they

---

44   Who am I kidding? I'm lucky if I can stick to it 80% of the time.

believe or worship exactly as they worship is lost and going to hell. Not only do some Christians cherish these beliefs, but they say them out loud to others while in line at the grocery store or when in front of a camera.

"Want to come to church with me? You should. Because if you don't, you're going to hell."

"Okay. Sounds like fun. Thanks for caring enough to ask."

What gives followers of Jesus the right to harbor in their hearts, much less display for others to see and hear, this kind of judgmental arrogance?

Nothing.

The Apostle Paul cuts the legs out from under all forms of Christian arrogance when he writes:

> As for you, you were dead in your transgressions and sins, in which you used to live when you followed the ways of this world. . . All of us also lived among them at one time, gratifying the cravings of our sinful nature and following its desires and thoughts. Like the rest, we were by nature objects of wrath. But because of his great love for us, God, who is rich in mercy, made us alive with Christ even when we were dead in transgressions. . .*For it is by grace you have been saved, through faith—and this not from yourselves, it is the gift of God—not by works, so that no one can boast.*[45]

We didn't invent the gospel. We didn't behave our way into salvation. We di   dn't do a single thing to earn our status as children of God. It was a gift from the Father. Pure grace.

---

45   Ephesians 2:8-10

It's when we lose touch with the gravity of grace and the immensity of God's love for us that Christian arrogance rears its ugly head.

Stay Grateful CrossFitting Christ-Followers

A couple of years ago I suffered a painful back injury while doing yoga in an effort to reduce nagging lower back pain.[46] The injury occurred just a few weeks before Sectionals of the CrossFit Games. I had no delusions of grandeur. I'm not a contender in any CrossFit competition I enter, but I enjoy the energy of participating in competitive events.

When I hurt my back, I was bummed for a couple of reasons. Not only was I going to miss competing, but I was also going to forfeit my entry fee. The only thing I hate more than missing a workout is wasting money. So I did everything imaginable to relieve my back pain so I could compete.

The week of the competition I found an online video demonstrating something called a "reverse-hyper." The guy in the video said it would do wonders for certain lower back injuries. I gave it a try and—miracle of miracles!—within two days my back was pain-free. I was able to compete. My performance that weekend was about what you'd expect from a guy in his late 30's with a bad back, but it didn't matter. I got my money's worth without doing any further damage to myself.

There was a camera crew at the competition capturing highlights on film. After my third WOD, one of the guys with a camera asked me how I felt about the workout I had just completed. When he asked, I was overwhelmed with a sense of gratitude. Within a span of just a few days I went from having no chance of competing to being able to complete a difficult

---

46   The only thing worse than chronic injuries are ironic injuries.

WOD that not everyone in my heat finished. All I could say to the camera was, "I'm just glad to be here. This was a gift. Pure grace."

On one hand, this is the kind of response you get when you ask a preacher who is too tired to edit himself to reflect on a CrossFit workout. I don't usually use theological language to describe a WOD. On the other hand, I said exactly what I felt in my heart. I was humbled by the opportunity to compete, I was grateful for the power of reverse-hypers to heal my back, and I believe all good gifts come from God.

There wasn't a hint of CrossFit arrogance in my heart that day, because gratitude and arrogance cannot co-exist with each other. It's impossible to look down on and judge others when you're aware of, and overwhelmed by, just how much of God's grace your life requires.

If more CrossFitters experienced the grace of God through CrossFit, and took the time to appreciate what a gift it is to be able to move fast, lift heavy, and eat clean, while also re-membering what life was like before CrossFit, it would change what we put on our T-shirts. It would also reverse the growing perception among outsiders that CrossFit creates great ath-letes and big jerks.

If more Christians experienced the grace of God through Christ (crazy thought I know), and spent more time reflect-ing on what a gift it is to be forgiven of our sins, filled with the Holy Spirit, and part of the family of God--in spite of our weaknesses, shortcomings, and sinful habits--it would change the way we treat our non-Christian neighbors. Perhaps this would change their attitude toward us and make them a bit more willing to listen when we put in a good word for Jesus.

Do you struggle with arrogance, either as a CrossFitter or a Christian?

What impact would gratitude have on your arrogance?

What are some ways you can begin to cultivate a spirit of thanksgiving?

You Are Not Your Fran Time

I have been crucified with Christ and I no longer live, but Christ lives in me. The life I now live in the body, I live by faith in the Son of God, who loved me and gave himself for me.

-Galatians 2:20 (NIV)

Making A Name For Ourselves

Here's a quick spiritual workout to try.

Read the following list out loud *as many times as necessary* (AMTAN) until you believe what it says.

Ready?

3-2-1 Go!

- I am not my Fran time.
- I am not my max snatch.
- I am not my ability to do a muscle-up.
- I am not the number of unbroken double unders I can do.
- I am not my body fat percentage.
- I am not my position on the CrossFit Open Leader Board.

- I am not my performance.
- I am not my achievements.
- I am not my resume.
- I am a child of God.
- I am created in the image of God.
- I am loved by God regardless of my Fran time, max snatch or body fat percentage.
- I am saved, forgiven, and empowered by the Holy Spirit because of what Christ accomplished on the cross, not because of what I have done.
- I am a new creation in Christ.

This may be the longest, hardest WOD we'll ever do. It'll take many of us a lifetime to successfully complete, because no matter how many times we work our way through this list, there will always be a part of us that struggles to believe that what we're reading out loud is true.

Just about every Christ-following CrossFitter I know struggles to manage the tension between being in love with a sport in which every second, rep, and pound counts and embracing a way of life in which our identity and self-worth is found in the risen Christ rather than in our performance.

This tension has been anchored deep in our psyche by a culture perpetually broadcasting the message that our achievements and our value as human beings are inextricably connected. Many of us heard this message at a young age and believed it. How could we do otherwise? The rewards for making good grades or excelling in sports were substantial.

It didn't take long to figure out that self-improvement was the key to capturing the attention of our parents, teachers, and coaches and essential to gaining popularity among our peers.

I remember when I discovered in junior high that being the best basketball player on the court was the secret to making my dreams come true. The more points I scored, the more compliments adults gave me and the more notes from cute girls were passed my way during class. In the eighth grade, my popularity skyrocketed because of basketball.

Throughout high school my identity was rooted in being a good basketball player. I took pride in being a four-year varsity starter, one of the leading scorers in the region, and for having the best free throw percentage in the state of Texas my senior year (91.9%).

It is unnecessary to share everything I just wrote in the previous sentence. Yet I felt compelled to include it because I desperately want everyone who reads this book to know that back in the day I was a legitimate athlete. I discovered CrossFit 10 years too late to be a great CrossFitter. I have to find other ways of validating my place in a roomful of fire-breathers. So I tell stories about the good ole days that pre-date Google and thus, can't be checked for accuracy.

Why do I find it necessary to do this? Because even though I've been a Christ-follower my entire life, I've always struggled to embrace the idea that my worth as a human being is determined by God's love for me and not my athletic performance.

There's a story in the Bible about a group of people who pool their wisdom, resources, and technology and start building a tower reaching into the heavens. Their motive for undertaking a project that God says is a bad idea? "So that we may make a name for ourselves."[47]

Some things never change.

---

47   Genesis 10:1-9

Our attempts to make a name for ourselves with our achievements stretch beyond ancient architecture and modern athletics. We can root our identity in our grade-point average, the number of people we slept with during college, how much money we make, the size of our house, the kind of car we drive, the label on our clothes, the level of knowledge and expertise we demonstrate in our work, and our religious activity.

One can argue that our desire to make a name for ourselves has led to countless achievements that have advanced our civilization and improved the human condition. One can also point to numerous examples of wildly successful people who are profoundly unhappy. Achievement is a great way to build a reputation, make money, and maybe even make the world a better place, but it's a shaky foundation on which to base an identity.

Justify My Existence

In the movie *Chariots of Fire*, Harold Abrahams is a great runner who finds little joy in his athletic achievements. Before an important race he says, "I will raise my eyes and look down that corridor; 4 feet wide, with 10 lonely seconds to justify my whole existence. But WILL I?"

He runs to justify his existence as a human being, and he is miserable.

There are a number of reasons why attempting to justify our existence with our performance leads to misery. Here are a few.

1. *Performance is relative.* There will always be someone smarter, richer, faster, stronger, and more popular than you. As long as you're measuring yourself against others, you'll

110

always be disappointed. Even if you reach the pinnacle of your field and become the richest, smartest, or fittest person in the world, it won't last forever, because...

2. *Performance is fleeting.* Charles Barkley likes to say "Father Time is undefeated." Even the best of all time get old and slow. There will always be a younger version of yourself breathing down your neck, ready to overtake and surpass your greatest achievements. Eventually we are all forced to talk about how great we used to be instead of letting our current performance speak for itself. At some point, you realize you're done setting PR's. Then what?

3. *Performance is addictive.* Like other addictions, we have to keep ramping up the stimuli in order to keep achieving a new and improved high. We max out our performance long before we hit the ceiling of being satisfied with our accomplishments. It's no accident that so many top performers turn to addictive substances to numb the pain from the nagging emptiness resulting from performing their best and still not feeling they've done enough to justify their existence.

Finding our identity in God's love as it's revealed through the life, death, and resurrection of Christ is a much better alternative than looking for it in the ebb and flow of our athletic performance. Again, there are several reasons why this is the case.

1. *God does not show favoritism.* We are not competing with others for God's love. He has an infinite supply, which he freely distributes. When our identity is rooted in Christ, we don't have to compare ourselves to others. We just have to stay focused on who we are in Christ.

2. *God's love is a universal constant.* It is the same yesterday, today, and tomorrow. As we grow older and wiser, our understanding of God's steadfast love increases. Our ability to appreciate and enjoy our identity in Christ gets better with age. Our best days as Christ-followers are always in front of us.

3. *God satisfies our deepest needs.* Saint Augustine wrote "Our heart is restless until it rests in you." Someone has paraphrased this by saying, "There is a God-shaped hole in our hearts." We'll never be able to fill it with our achievements. Only God can give us the peace and contentment we're seeking.

The Secret

In one of his letters the Apostle Paul writes about the way his attitude toward his achievements changed after his encounter with the risen Christ. He says:

> If someone else thinks he has reasons to put confidence in the flesh, I have more: circumcised on the eighth day, of the people of Israel, of the tribe of Benjamin, a Hebrew of Hebrews; in regard to the law, a Pharisee; as for zeal, persecuting the church; as for legalistic righteousness, faultless. But whatever was to my profit I now consider loss for the sake of Christ. *What is more, I consider everything a loss compared to the surpassing greatness of knowing Christ Jesus my Lord, for whose sake I have lost all things. I consider them rubbish, that I may gain Christ and be found in him,* not having a righteousness of my own that comes from the law, but that which is through faith in Christ— the righteousness that comes from God and is by faith.[48]

As far as religious resumes go, Paul's was hard to beat. He's not exaggerating his pedigree, his passion, or his performance.

---

48   Philippians 3:4-9

He was that good. His new identity in Christ changed the way he regarded himself and his religious activity. He says his past accomplishments are rubbish[49] compared to knowing Christ.

He is not his family tree. He is not his credentials. He is not his achievements. He is a follower of Christ who longs to identify with the resurrected Christ as fully as possible, even if it means suffering and dying as Christ did.

Later on in the same letter he writes:

> . . .I have learned to be content whatever the circumstances. I know what it is to be in need, and I know what it is to have plenty. I have learned the secret of being content in any and every situation, whether well fed or hungry, whether living in plenty or in want. I can do everything through him who gives me strength.[50]

At the end of this little passage is one of the most misapplied verses in all of Scripture. When Paul says, "I can do everything (or all things) through him who gives me strength," he's not saying that Christ gives him ability to run a four-minute mile, deadlift 600 pounds, or leap tall buildings with a single bound. He's saying that Christ has given him the ability to be content in all circumstances, regardless of the outcome.

In the context of the letter, he's talking about having enough money to survive. His point is that his sense of well-being isn't dependent on his possessions. He calls this the "secret to being content." His secret is that his identity in Christ trumps his external circumstances.

---

49   The word Paul uses here is literally translated "dung." He says his past accomplishments aren't worth crap compared to knowing Christ. Put that on a magnet and stick it to your refrigerator door.
50   Philippians 4:11-13. I don't blame you if you would rather stick this verse to your refrigerator.

Here's a CrossFitter's paraphrase of this passage:

I have learned to be content in CrossFit. I know what it's like to have a terrible workout and I know what it's like to set a gym record. I have learned the secret to being content in every situation, whether standing on the podium or lying flat on my back in defeat, whether exceeding my expectations on a WOD or turning in a disappointing performance. I can be content in all these circumstances because my identity in Christ trumps my athletic achievements, or lack thereof.

Does this mean we shouldn't pursue personal and gym records and strive for CrossFit greatness? Not at all. Having our identity firmly established in Christ sets us free to enjoy God through CrossFit.

Eric Liddell is another runner whose story is told in *Chariots of Fire*. He's a missionary from Scotland. When debating with his sister about whether he should compete he says, "I believe God made me for a purpose, but he also made me fast. And when I run I feel His pleasure."

When our identity is rooted in the universal constant of God's love, we can chase greatness knowing that our successes and our failures have absolutely no bearing on our identity in Christ. This is the difference between running to justify our existence and running to feel the pleasure of God at work within us. It's also the difference between enjoying life and being miserable.

The Whiteboard

I love the whiteboard. It's one of the features of CrossFit that initially drew me in. The whiteboard invites competition. It increases accountability. It asks us to take responsibility for our performance.

I also like how the whiteboard is erasable. There is a valuable lesson in having the results of our blood, sweat, and blisters disappear before our eyes with one swipe from a damp towel.

What we do in the gym matters. It's important enough to put next to our name. Our performance can inspire others to dig deeper and work harder. But it's wise to remember that at the end of the day, it all gets erased.

Please don't write on your heart what can be so easily erased from a whiteboard.

You are not your Fran time.

Your existence was justified when the Father created you.

Your value was established when Jesus died for you.

Your new identity was sealed when the Spirit filled you.

You are a new creation in Christ.

Let God's love write this on your heart with a permanent marker.

Conclusion: For The Sake Of Others

Instead, whoever wants to become great among you must be your servant, and whoever wants to be first must be slave of all. For even the Son of Man did not come to be served, but to serve, and to give his life as a ransom for many.

-Mark 10:43-45 (NIV)

A Dangerous Obsession

It's easy to get sucked into the vortex of constant and never-ending improvement at the heart of CrossFit. The workouts are potent. The results are motivating. The community never stops encouraging us to keep pushing ourselves to the next level.

This Kool-Aid doesn't kill you; it makes you stronger, faster, leaner, and meaner.

As far as obsessions go, we can do much worse than CrossFit. Even so, obsessions are dangerous, because they almost always turn inward and become selfish endeavors pursued at the expense of others.

If your dedication to eating clean is making those around you more uncomfortable than it is making you, you're not doing it right. If while eating with friends at a restaurant, you pull out a scale and start measuring your food, you deserve to eat alone.

When a friend shares some great news about a new job, love interest, or addition to his family, if you try to one up him with the news of how you knocked one second off of your Fran time earlier that day, be ready to duck, or find a new friend.

You keep saying that the next big CrossFit competition isn't more important than your family. Yet they repeatedly have to make do with the traces of time and energy you have left at the end of each training day.

There is an old-fashioned religious word for turning something good into a harmful obsession: idolatry.

CrossFit is a breeding ground for idolatrous attachments. But then again, so is religion.

In our pursuit of spiritual fitness, we can become obsessed with exercises like prayer, meditation, Bible study, worship, and serving others. Like all other obsessions, our spiritual training can turn inward and become a selfish pursuit. Religion is the most dangerous idol of all because it comes disguised in the cloak of (self) righteousness.

Religious idolaters practice spiritual exercises not in an effort to connect with God, but to feel superior to others. They serve the needy not with a loving heart, but with a guilty conscience, hoping their good deeds will take away the pain from past mistakes. They fill their calendars with religious activity to improve their chances of going to heaven when they die, or to have something to brag about at parties. When writing paragraphs like this one, religious idolaters use "they" instead of "we."

One antidote to the idolatry of physical or spiritual fitness comes from developing the biggest answer possible to the question: Why do we train?

We train physically for a number of reasons, some more noble than others: to feel better, to look better, to live longer, to make friends, or to win. The reasons for training spiritually are just as diverse in scope and motive.

One of the best reasons is usually one of the last to come to mind.

Be Strong To Be Useful

On May 8, 1902, the town of Saint-Pierre, Martinique, was overwhelmed by the volcanic eruption of nearby Mount Pelee. Georges Hébert, a French soldier stationed on the island, coordinated the rescue and escape of over 700 people.

His experience reinforced his belief that athletic skill was meant to be used in combination with courage and service. He coined the slogan "be strong to be useful" to express this conviction. He later used obstacle courses to train his fellow soldiers. His approach to fitness became known as *parkour* and "be strong to be useful" continues to be a guiding principle for the modern day parkour community.

Not long ago, a group of CrossFitters from area boxes got together to help an elderly woman move. Over her lifetime she accumulated several truckloads of heaviness. As we deadlifted boxes of books (or was it bricks?) and clean and jerked furniture made of solid wood (or was it cement?), there was great satisfaction in knowing that this is why we train; so that our fitness can be useful to others.

Jesus taught his early followers that the best motive for wanting to be more like him wasn't to become great, but to become servants. This is how we keep our physical and spiritual training from becoming idols. We train our bodies, minds, and spirits to be useful in the service of others.

Why We Train

I recently re-watched the HBO mini-series *Band of Brothers* on DVD. It tells the story of the men from Easy Company of the U. S. Army 101st Airborne division. It begins with their paratrooper training at Camp Toccoa, Georgia and follows them all the way to Hitler's Eagle's Nest in Bavaria at the end of the war.

Every episode is good, but perhaps the best, and certainly the most difficult to watch, is entitled *Why We Fight*.

Throughout the episode, different characters debate the meaning of the war as its end approaches. Why are we here? What was our purpose? Was this a waste of time and lives?

Near the end of the episode they discover a concentration camp just outside of a German village. The camp guards have abandoned their posts and left the emaciated prisoners to die. Easy Company liberates the prisoners and forces the citizens of the nearby village to bury the dead.

The camp's existence is the answer to their questions. This is why we're here. This is why we've made these sacrifices. This is why we fight.

They were there for the sake of others who couldn't fight for themselves.

Even if not immediately obvious, there is a higher purpose for our existence. There is a reason to train for physical and spiritual fitness that goes deeper and reaches higher than the selfish motives that keep us teetering on the brink of idolatry.

Someday this reason will be revealed and we will know why we train.

Because someday, someone will need you to be. . .

Better and stronger than you are right now.

Capable of a deeper love, full of more courage, ready to exercise more faith, and able to show more grace than you have right now.

And more ready for anything than you are right now.

Be strong to be useful, for the sake of others.

This is why we train.

Appendix One: Spiritual Fitness In 100 Words

For the Spirit God gave us does not make us timid, but gives us power, love and self-discipline.

-2 Timothy 1:7 (NIV)

By now, you've hopefully started thinking about what your spiritual training program will look like. As you do this, I recommend you spend some time developing a summary of your plan, also known as a "rule of life."[51]

A rule of life should be succinct, realistic, and motivating.

Coach Glassman's *World Class Fitness in 100 Words* is an excellent example of a rule of life for physical fitness:

Eat meat and vegetables, nuts and seeds, some fruit, little starch and no sugar. Keep intake to levels that will support exercise but not body fat. Practice and train major lifts: deadlift, clean, squat, presses, clean & jerk, and snatch. Similarly, master the basics of gymnastics: pull-ups, dips, rope climb, push-ups, sit-ups, presses to handstand, pirouettes, flips,

---

51 For more on how to develop a rule of life, check out Chapter 9 in *Soul Feast* by Marjorie J. Thompson..

splits, and holds. Bike, run, swim, row, etc, hard and fast. Five or six days per week mix these elements in as many combinations and patterns as creativity will allow. Routine is the enemy. Keep workouts short and intense. Regularly learn and play new sports.
—Greg Glassman

The genius of this summary is that it captures the basics of CrossFit in one paragraph. Every sentence can be expanded into a multi-day seminar and some of the skills mentioned require a lifetime to master. But it can all be summarized in 100 words.

Here's an exercise to try: write your own version of "Spiritual Fitness in 100 Words."

As you do, consider these three questions:

1. What spiritual exercises am I attracted to and why?
2. Where do I feel God calling me to stretch and grow?
3. What kind of balance do I need in my life?

"Athletes, musicians, writers, scientists, and others progress in their fields because they are well-disciplined people. Unfortunately, there is a tendency to think that in matters of faith we should pray, meditate, and engage in other spiritual disciplines only when we feel like it."
-William Paulsell

A good rule of life will lean into our strengths, remind us to train our weaknesses, and take into account our season of life. Each rule of life is as unique as the personality, gifts, and circumstances of the one who writes it.

Here's my own version of Spiritual Fitness in 100 Words:

Start with grace. Practice humility. Ask big questions. Love others with your words AND your actions. Break bread with people who aren't like you. Move toward your fears. Be hyper-sensitive to arrogance and entitlement in yourself. Be quick to forgive the faults you see in others. Pray for others more than you pray for yourself. Bounce your eyes and take every thought captive. Identify your idols by paying attention to what makes you anxious. Be a "little christ" everywhere you go. Say "thank you," "that's enough," and "you're welcome" every day. Read. Listen. Fast. Work. Rest. Play. End with grace.[52]

Now it's time to work on yours.

If you'd like to share what you come up with, send it to wadehodges@gmail.com.

---

52   100 words, right on the money! But I'm not a legalist. I counted hyper-sensitive as one word by the way. Still not a legalist though.

Appendix Two: The Gospel Story

I am not ashamed of the gospel, because it is the power of
God that brings salvation to everyone who believes. . .

-Romans 1:16 (NIV)

I've assumed that readers of this book have a basic understanding of the gospel story told in Scripture. To make sure
we're on the same page, I'm including a brief summary of the
story below. Just to be clear: if it isn't done in response to the
gospel, all the spiritual training in the world isn't going to help
us overcome the fundamental problems of sin and death.

The Story From Above

The Bible is a long book that seems to tell a pretty complicated story, spanning thousands of years, written in three lan-
guages, with hundreds of characters with hard to pronounce
names. Yet on the other side of this complexity is a plot so
simple it's stunning. At its heart, the Bible tells a story of good
news about God and God's world. We call this good news story
"The Gospel."

The gospel story can be summarized in a number of ways. It all
depends on the perspective from which the story gets told and
the point from where we choose to start the telling. We usually

start with our problems and needs and what the gospel story has to offer people like us. How does the gospel benefit us? What can we get out of this story? These are the questions we want to have answered above all others.

These questions have their place and we'll get around to answering them, but they're not the best place to start the story. Instead, let's start with where the Bible starts.

"In the beginning, God[53] . . ."

The gospel story starts (and ends) with God. He's more than the main character. He's the author who writes himself into the story. So it makes sense to ask, "What is the gospel from God's perspective? What is God up to in this story? What kind of story is God telling?" Once we start seeing the gospel story from God's perspective we can then better appreciate the story from our perspective.

It's crucial to get this order right. It will change the way we see God, the world, and our place within the story. Rather than asking *How does God fit into my life and what I'm doing?* let's ask *How does my life fit into God and what God is doing in the world?*

So here's a summary of the gospel from God's perspective, or at least it's the best we can do to piece together what the Bible says about how God views the world. If we were able to see everything from God's perspective, it would break our hearts, blow our minds, and leave us more devastated than six rounds of Fight Gone Bad.

---

53   Genesis 1:1

For summary purposes we can break the story up into three major scenes.

Scene 1: Creation and Fall

In the beginning, God created everything you can see and everything you can't. God's creative activity was a labor of love and God loved what he created. When he finished God said, "This is good, very good." And it was good. Creation was at peace. There was a sense of wholeness. Cosmic harmony. "Shalom" is the fancy word for this.

Human beings are God's favorite part of creation. He created them, both male and female, in his image. By creating humanity in his image, God gives them the ability to love God and each other and to exercise God's authority in the world. Humanity is created to be God's partners in loving and caring for creation, while continuing to create good things in the world.

God also gives human beings the freedom to think for themselves and make their own choices. Faster than you can say "big mistake," they use their freedom to rebel against God. They go their own way and evil enters the world. Some call this act of rebellion "The Fall."

The result is that God's good world is broken in every way imaginable. The image of God in humanity is scarred and distorted by the forces of evil. Love and community give way to selfishness and violence. Human creativity develops a self-serving shadow. The earth is cursed and groans under the weight of the burden. Shalom is destroyed.

What was once very good goes bad in a hurry and God allows it to happen. But that doesn't mean God is content to leave his broken world in a state of disrepair. God loves his world too much to sit back and watch it spin completely out of control.

Scene 2: Redemption

God sets a plan in motion to reverse the curse that has come upon his creation. Just as God created humanity to be his partners in caring for creation, he also partners with humanity for the purposes of redemption.

He invites Abraham and his family to be his partners in bringing a blessing to the world. He partners with a prophet named Moses to help Israel (Abraham's family) become a light in a dark world. He partners with famous people like King David and with people we've never heard of.

It's a beautiful plan, but it has a fatal flaw. God's partners keep failing to uphold their end of the deal. They can't break free from the forces of evil that have enslaved them. They continue to rebel against God even as he tries to save them.

Since God can't find a suitable human partner, God enters the story as a human being--Jesus Christ.[54]

In Christ, God comes into the world to defeat the forces of evil and restore the image of God in humanity. This is what we see Jesus doing through his life, death, and resurrection. We'll talk more about the specifics of what Jesus did and how he did it later on.

Scene 3. Restoration/Recreation

Jesus is the catalyst that sets off a chain reaction in the world that will eventually bring about a complete restoration of God's

---

54   The fancy word for the idea that God became human is "Incarnation."

creation. What was broken in the fall will be repaired. Evil will be extinguished once and for all. The gospel story ends with God's broken, but still good world being transformed into a new heavens and new earth. In the end, shalom will once again be the norm for God's world.

In each of these three scenes, God is the star of the show. He does all the heavy lifting and gets all the credit. He creates, redeems, forgives, heals, restores, and repairs. As the star, God lets his beauty, creativity, faithfulness, wisdom, strength, mercy, grace, and his glory shine into the darkness so that his world can be healed and so that his favorite part of creation can be saved.

From this top-down perspective, the gospel is a story about a God who will stop at nothing to overcome human rebellion and defeat the forces of evil in order to put his broken world back together again.

Now let's reverse the angle and tell the gospel story from the bottom-up.

The Story From Below

In the Ancient Near East--the time and place out of which much of the Bible was written--kings often erected statues of themselves in far flung corners of their empires. These statues were intended to represent the king in his absence. The statue continually reminded the people who was in charge. In a similar way, our creator placed us in the world, made in his image, to rule the earth on his behalf.

In the beginning God created the world and saw that it was very good. We were created to live in harmony with God, each other, the world, and ourselves.

We started out with so much potential. But our desire to live independently of God messed up everything in all directions. Creation comes under a curse. The impact of our rebellion impairs our ability to experience meaningful relationships in all areas of life.[55]

Our sin, which is a religious word for our rebellion against God, alienated us from God. A relationship once held together by intimacy, trust, and friendship is shattered by fear, anxiety, and misunderstanding. In shame, we hide from the one who knows us best and loves us the most.

Our sin also alienated us from each other. We can't seem to relate to each other in positive ways even when we want to. We were created to live in community with others and yet we end up sabotaging it every time we get within sniffing distance of anything resembling a healthy relationship. One of our greatest fears is to be left alone, but at the same time we can't stand the thought of someone getting too close.

Our sin has also alienated us from the rest of creation. God entrusted his world--the rivers, oceans, mountains, prairies, forests, deserts and all that lives within them--to us and we have not done well with it. Instead of taking care of God's world we've exploited, polluted, and destroyed beautiful chunks of it.

We've managed to take everything that's good about creation and pervert, abuse, and misuse it. Food is good, but we eat ourselves to death. Creativity is good, but we've created just as many ways to kill each other as to help each other. Sex is good, but we find it almost impossible to experience its goodness without being consumed by it.

---

55   Read Genesis 3 to get the details.

Finally, our sin brought about self-alienation or shame. Shame and guilt are two different feelings. We feel guilty because we do something wrong. We experience shame when we believe there is something wrong with us. Most of us have in our minds an ideal of what it means to be a "good" person and we consistently fall short of our own standards. Our consistent inconsistency compounds our shame, which usually resides on levels so deep in our psyche that we are unaware of how it impacts our ability to relate with others. It's hard to imagine that we're loved by God or other people, and it's hard to show love to others, when deep inside we hate ourselves.

We're still capable of goodness, of course, because the image of God has not completely left us. But we find it impossible to be consistently good. We can do something beautiful in a flash of inspiration and then 10 minutes later do something awful. We can do good while harboring terrible feelings inside about the good we're doing and we can do terrible things while thinking about how much we'd love to be doing something good. We are walking contradictions.

So we find ourselves in a big mess of our own making. The harder we try to make things better, the worse we make them. Even when we do the right thing, we do it in the wrong way, for the wrong reason, at the wrong time and end up doing more harm than good.

The heavier the burden of our guilt and shame becomes, the worse we feel about ourselves. This increases the likelihood of destructive behavior, which compounds our our guilt and shame.

Lurking behind all of this is a sense of dread coming from the knowledge of our impending death. We know that death comes for us all, but we have no idea what comes after death. The more we think about our coming death the more meaningless our present life seems. What's the point of life if we all end up dead anyway?[56]

We're in quite a predicament aren't we?

There is an old story about a stork who finds himself stuck in a deep bog of mud. The stork furiously flaps its wings trying to break free but can't. To gain leverage, the stork puts his beak into the mud and manages to pull out one foot and then the other, only to realize that now its beak has sunk too deep in the mud to be extracted. So he puts one foot down and then the other hoping to gain some leverage. . .

That's our story. We're stuck in the mud and we can't get out. Our best efforts only make things worse. In fact, the harder we try to break free, the deeper we sink.

The truth is we'll never free ourselves from the compounding consequences of our sin. Someone else will have to come along and get us out of the mess we're in. It's only after we finally accept this reality that the gospel story starts to make sense from our perspective.

The gospel is the story of how God comes to rescue us from ourselves, our sin, and from the forces of evil that have taken advantage of our rebellious spirits and enslaved us.

Jesus joins us in the mud, gets stuck in our mess, and gives us the leverage we need to break free. The gospel is good news because Jesus has come to do what we can't do for ourselves.

The name Jesus means "God saves." Jesus is our salvation. In the gospel story, salvation can have a number of meanings.

---

56   Read Ecclesiastes if you want to follow this depressing thought all the way to the bottom of hope.

Salvation means our sins are forgiven and our relationship with God is restored. God takes away our guilt and shame and replaces it with his loving presence (aka the Holy Spirit). God lives in us and we live in God.

Salvation means broken community can be repaired. Jesus teaches us to love, serve and forgive others so we can live in harmony with each other.

Salvation means we are equipped to do the job we were originally created to do. Jesus gives us wisdom so we can be good stewards of the world that God has entrusted to us and better reflect God's image back into his creation.

Salvation means death is not the end of our story. It means the good we do in this life is not wasted or forgotten. When God finally renews and restores his creation, we will be raised to life so we can enjoy God and each other in God's good world—forever.

This is all made possible by what God has done through the life, death, and resurrection of Jesus.

So from our perspective, we can say that the gospel is a story about how God comes to rescue us and present us with a benefit package filled with more blessings than we can count.

But the gospel is more than just a benefit package. It's also a job description. Just as God made us in his image to be his creative partners in caring for the world, he also saves us so that we can partner with him in repairing and restoring what is broken.

Do you see why gospel means good news?

The gospel is good news about God: There is no end to his love. He will not be denied. He will put his broken world back together again even if it kills him (and it did).

It's good news about the world: God is putting his broken world back together one person at a time.

It's good news about us: God loves us so much that he has come to save us and include us in his story of redemption. He offers us a job description and an unbeatable benefit package to go with it.

Finally, it's good news about Jesus: He is the victorious Lord who conquered sin, death, and the forces of evil. None of this would even be news, much less good news, if it weren't for his life, death, and resurrection. Jesus is the center of the story from both perspectives.

Jesus: The Center Of The Story

Whether we begin telling the gospel story from God's perspective or from ours, we'll end up at the same place: Jesus. He brings both perspectives of the story together and holds them in place until God's glory is revealed and we are rescued from our trouble.

Until Jesus, God has been a character without a face. At different times in the Bible, God is revealed as a force or a presence or a voice, but it's not until Jesus appears as one of us that we are able to understand what God is really like. In Jesus, God's faithfulness and humanity's frailty become one. The result is salvation with its promise of a new creation with new life, new hope, and new opportunities.

We get a better understanding of what this means by reading the Gospels—the four books in the New Testament known as Matthew, Mark, Luke, and John. They're like highlight reels of Jesus' life showing us how his life, death, and resurrection are central to the gospel story.

His Life
Jesus was born into scandal. He grew up in obscurity. Then one day he stepped onto history's stage and changed everything. He came preaching a message about "The Kingdom of God." This was the message of liberation the world had been waiting to hear. But he didn't come merely to talk about or explain the kingdom. He came to embody it. As powerful as his teachings were, they were nothing compared to the grace and truth demonstrated by his actions.

He healed the sick, raised the dead, and cast evil spirits out of people as a way of demonstrating God's intention to heal and restore his entire creation. Jesus spent time with "sinners"—those who had been excluded by the religious elite—as a way of showing that no person, no matter how messy his or her life, was beyond the reach of God's forgiving love.

He spoke words of truth to those who had lost their way or had been led astray. He called people to repent, to change their thinking and their actions, in response to his message. He demonstrated a way of life befitting human beings created in the image of God.

To those who were paying attention and really listening to what he had to say, he revealed an alternative path unlike anything offered by his contemporaries. He invited a select group of people to be his "disciples" or "apprentices." They followed him closely and learned this new way of life from him so they could someday pass it on to others. Jesus began a revolution of love, grace, and truth that would eventually reach the ends of the earth and include people from all nations.

All of this was supposed to be good news, but many who heard Jesus teach didn't receive it as such. He accumulated enemies just as quickly as he gathered followers. It was the religious leaders who had the biggest problem with him. He challenged their traditions and embarrassed them by accepting sinners they had rejected. He undermined their influence with his authoritative teaching style. He condemned their religious institutions, like the temple in Jerusalem, that were doing more harm than good. They were also jealous of him. The crowds were paying too much attention to everything he said and did.

These crowds were also a threat to the Roman Empire. Nothing made "the powers that be" more nervous than a charismatic leader who could build a following and motivate the people to action. Rome didn't tolerate revolutionaries. That is exactly what the religious leaders made Jesus out to be to the Roman authorities. Of course, Jesus was leading a revolution, but it wasn't a revolution advanced with swords and clubs. It was a revolution of love. But this didn't matter to Rome.

The crowds around Jesus were large; they were also fickle. It happened in Jerusalem at the time of Passover, a season of intense religious and political fervor. Jesus' enemies whipped into a frenzy the same people, who just a few days earlier, had given Jesus a hero's welcome into town. They convinced Pilate, the Roman governor, that the best way to keep the peace was to execute Jesus by crucifixion.

His Death
The crucifixion of Jesus was history's darkest moment. Not just because a righteous man died an excruciating death he didn't deserve, but also because it appeared that once again the forces of evil had thwarted God's attempt to rescue his creation. As it turned out, the cross was actually the best, and most unexpected

plot twist in the history of storytelling. Had we been there to witness those six brutal hours Jesus spent on the cross, in addition to the torture he endured before the crucifixion, we would have seen nothing significant in his death. He would have looked just like any other failed Messiah who had come to Jerusalem with delusions of grandeur and ended up on a cross.

Yet, the Christian faith is built on the conviction that something cosmically significant was happening as Jesus died on the cross. Somehow, in some way, while on the cross Jesus was fighting the ultimate battle against evil, on our behalf. The forces of evil threw everything they had at Jesus and he absorbed it all. The worst of the human condition—betrayal, jealousy, guilt, shame, fear, doubt, isolation, and brokenness--was placed upon his shoulders. By taking all of this upon himself, Jesus made a way for us to step out from under the burden of our guilt and shame, while freeing us from the grip of evil, which had enslaved us to sin and death.

Sometimes an image helps us understand Jesus' death in a way that words can't. Imagine a mother hen gathering her chicks under her wings as a prairie fire rages across a farm. As the fire passes, the chicks are protected from the flames as their mother takes the full force of the heat upon herself. Her death makes life possible for others.[57]

Jesus' death does more than just save us from evil. It also reverses the curse brought about by the fall and restores our broken relationships. By showing us pure love in action, Jesus draws us back into relationship with God and shows us how to relate with others. From the cross, Jesus shows us what God really looks like. Having seen the face of unconditional, self-giving, sacrificial love, we see everything else in a different

---

57   Thanks to N. T. Wright, my theological hero, for this image.

light as well. When we become a part of God's story and learn to love as Jesus loved, it opens up an entirely different--and much better--way of relating to and experiencing the joys found in the world around us. His death gives us life.

His Resurrection
How can we believe that what I've just described isn't just the product of a bad case of wishful thinking? How do we know that something significant happened when Jesus died on the cross? The death of Jesus is meaningful for only one reason—the resurrection.

After Jesus was killed on the cross, his body was placed in a tomb. After three days, on a Sunday, the Gospels report that Jesus was raised from the dead and appeared to his disciples. The Christian faith stands or falls on whether the resurrection actually happened. If Jesus wasn't raised from the dead, then he was a failed messiah who was really no different than all the other wandering sages of his day.

If he was raised from the dead, and there is good reason to believe that he was, then everything he said and did takes on greater weight. The resurrection elevates Jesus from the status of a good teacher and doer of good deeds to the Lord of all creation and the author of salvation. The resurrection validates Jesus' identity as the Son of God and vindicates everything he said. The resurrection is God's way of saying, "This is my son, whom I love, listen to him!"

The resurrection is also God's way of declaring an irrefutable victory over the forces of evil. Jesus entered the shadowy world of sin and death and emerged from his tomb victorious. This is good news because if sin and death have no power over

Jesus, then they have no lasting power over those who are "in Christ."[58]

While there aren't enough words in any language to adequately explain the logic and process of how we are saved by Jesus, the historic Christian conviction is that our sins are forgiven, evil is defeated, creation is restored, and the light of God's glory shines most brightly through the life, death, and resurrection of Jesus. There simply would be no good news story to tell without him.

To grasp the difference Jesus can make in our lives takes a lifetime of exploration. A kind of exploration done not so much by reading books, but by becoming a part of God's story and learning how to live, love, and die as Jesus did.

Becoming Part Of The Story

The gospel is a story unlike any other. Its purpose is not merely to entertain us or to tell us what happened a long time ago or to give us something interesting to talk about with others. The gospel story ends with an invitation which calls for a response from everyone who hears it.

Some never get far enough into the story to hear the invitation. Others hear it and reject it or misunderstand it. Some hear it, accept it and are transformed.

When we accept the invitation we experience what is called a "conversion." When converted we experience the joy of salvation. We start seeing our life in light of what God is doing in the world through the gospel. We start thinking of ourselves

---

58   "In Christ" is one of the most important little phrases in the Bible. Read Ephesians 1:3-14 and note all the blessings associated with being "in Christ."

as God's partners in repairing his broken world. To be converted is to become a part of God's story.

What does conversion look like? How does it happen? How do we formally accept the benefit package and agree to start fulfilling the job description offered to us by the gospel?

How To Respond
There are a number of stories in Acts describing how different people become followers of Christ.[59] While each story is as different as the person being converted, each story has several common elements.

The gospel story is told. There is an explanation of what God has done through the life, death, and resurrection of Jesus.

Those who hear the story are faced with a choice: What do I do with this story about the resurrected Jesus? Some reject it or ignore it, but others believe it. They believe that Jesus was raised from the dead and they believe that this means they can be saved, forgiven, and restored. Their belief (or faith) compels them to change the way they're living.

This change is called repentance. To repent means to change directions. Repentance involves a change in both thought and action. Faith that doesn't lead to repentance is no faith at all. Those who embrace the gospel will see their lives change in noticeable ways.

In Acts, those who embrace the gospel story express their faith through baptism. They are immersed in water.

---

59   You might want to go read several of them now. Here's where to start: Acts 2:36-47; 8:26-39; 16:25-34; 22:6-16.

Those who respond to the gospel with faith, repentance, and baptism are also committing the rest of their lives to learning and practicing the ways of Jesus (training for Christ-likeness). The longer they follow Jesus by obeying his teachings and imitating his example, the more like Jesus they become. This process is called "spiritual formation" and you can read more about how it works in Appendix Three.

Appendix Three: A Brief Introduction To Spiritual Formation

Do not be deceived: God cannot be mocked. A man reaps what he sows. Whoever sows to please their flesh, from the flesh will reap destruction; whoever sows to please the Spirit, from the Spirit will reap eternal life. Let us not become weary in doing good, for at the proper time we will reap a harvest if we do not give up.

-Galatians 6:7-9 (NIV)

Spiritual Formation

One of my favorite traits of the CrossFit community is the fascination with the theory behind the programming and the willingness to dive into the science behind the workouts. If you've attended a Level 1 Certification, watched a video of Coach Glassman lecturing, or read an article in the CrossFit Journal, you have been exposed to dense, wordy sentences and complex diagrams explaining how and why CrossFit works the way it does. You don't have to understand all the technical language to reap the benefits from CrossFit, but if you're the kind of person who loves to dig deeper, the CrossFit community provides the resources to take you as far down as you want to go.

In the same way, I want to offer a brief, but slightly technical discussion of some of the theology undergirding this project.

I've emphasized the necessity of training for spiritual fitness (Christ-likeness). The process of becoming more like Christ is called "spiritual formation" or "discipleship" or "sanctification" depending on the theological background of the one leading the discussion. I'm partial to "spiritual formation," but comfortable with the other terms as well.

The language of spiritual formation comes from several images the Apostle Paul uses in his letters.

"My dear children, for whom I am again in the pains of childbirth until Christ is formed in you, . . ." (Galatians 4:19)

Until Christ is formed in you--Like a baby growing in the womb, Christ is growing in us. It's a weird image, especially if you're a man, but with a little imagination we can make it work.

"For those God foreknew he also predestined to be conformed to the likeness of his Son, that he might be the firstborn among many brothers." (Romans 8:29)

Conformed to the likeness of his Son—We are molded and shaped into the image of Christ, our older brother.

"And we, who with unveiled faces all reflect the Lord's glory, are being transformed into his likeness with ever-increasing glory, which comes from the Lord, who is the Spirit." (2 Corinthians 3:18)

Being transformed into his likeness—Just as a caterpillar is transformed into a butterfly, sinners are transformed into saints by the power of the Holy Spirit.

How Spiritual Formation Works

So how does spiritual formation happen? How do we progressively become more like Christ over the course of a lifetime?

It doesn't happen automatically or accidentally. We don't wake up having experienced a Pinocchio-like transformation overnight, at least not until our resurrection, and that's the end of our transformation, not the beginning.

It's not the result of asking, "What would Jesus do?" every time we face a tough decision. Many times it's easier to ask the question than to know what Jesus would actually do in a given situation.

The process of becoming more like Christ is more complicated and nuanced than we might initially assume.

It begins with an invitation from Jesus to follow him, to imitate him, and to learn from him the secrets of the Kingdom of God. Jesus doesn't force himself on anyone. God doesn't coerce us into Christ-likeness. It's important to remember that.

Those who accept the invitation discover spiritual formation to be a mysterious combination of God's power and our intentional activity (spiritual training) resulting in a changed life. Like so many other aspects of the gospel, God asks us to partner with him in the process of becoming more like Christ.

That last paragraph will make some people uncomfortable. In some Christian circles, there is a false dichotomy between

God's grace and human effort. Mention our activity, work, or effort in connection with the gospel and you can count on someone throwing a heresy flag while accusing you of promoting "works righteousness" or legalism. While I understand the concern, I reject the either/or thinking behind it that says, "If we are saved by grace then our effort toward transformation is unnecessary."

It is true that we can do nothing to earn God's favor. His love comes with no strings attached. His grace is a free gift made possible through the life, death, and resurrection of Jesus. But God's grace does not nullify human effort as a necessary response to God's grace in the spiritual formation process.

God's grace transforms us; we must participate in our own transformation. This is but one of many tensions followers of Jesus must embrace if we are to fully participate in the gospel story.

The connection between God's power to change us and our effort is captured beautifully in a passage written by the Apostle Peter, a guy who knew a thing or two about it taking a lifetime to become more like Christ. Pay special attention to the words I've put in bold:

> His **divine power has given us everything we need for life and godliness** through our knowledge of him who called us by his own glory and goodness. Through these he has given us his very great and precious promises, so that through them you may **participate in the divine nature** and escape the corruption in the world caused by evil desires. For this very reason, **make every effort** to add to your faith goodness; and to goodness, knowledge; and to knowledge, self- control; and to self-control, perseverance; and to perseverance, godliness; and to godliness, brotherly

kindness; and to brotherly kindness, love. For if you possess these qualities in increasing measure, they will keep you from **being ineffective and unproductive in your knowledge of our Lord Jesus Christ.** But **if anyone does not have them, he is nearsighted and blind, and has forgotten that he has been cleansed from his past sins.**[60]

Several observations from this passage:

1. God supplies the power for our transformation. He gives us everything we need to grow in Christ-likeness. Spiritual formation is a work the Holy Spirit does in us. God forms Christ in us. God is the potter in whose hands we are conformed to the image of Christ. God transforms us from big sinners into *little christs*.

2. Our response to the grace of God, manifested in the call to a new way of life in Christ, is to "make every effort" to cultivate the virtues of Christ-likeness in our character. The Apostle Paul calls this "training for godliness."[61] We've been calling it "pursuing spiritual fitness."

3. If we claim to follow Christ and yet are not actively cultivating these virtues in our lives, it is a sign we have lost sight of the grace that forgave our sins and called us into a new way of life in the first place.

These same thoughts are echoed when the Apostle Paul writes:

Therefore, I urge you, brothers and sisters, in view of God's mercy, to offer your bodies as a living sacrifice, holy and pleasing to God—this is true worship. Do not conform to

---

60   2 Peter 1:3-9
61   1 Timothy 4:8; 1 Corinthians 9:24-25

the pattern of this world, but be transformed by the renewing of your mind. Then you will be able to test and approve what God's will is—his good, pleasing and perfect will.[62]

Again, our response to the mercy of God is to submit our lives to the transforming power of God.

The order is important: God moves first through the gospel, then we respond by showing up and opening up. We "show up" when we submit our lives to the will and power of God and we "open up" when we say, "God I'm ready and willing to learn whatever it is you want to teach me."

Spiritual training, as I've described it in this book, is the daily act of opening up our lives to the power of God by engaging in a variety of exercises across multiple spiritual domains. These exercises are not necessary for God to be able to do his work. Rather, they're necessary for our participation in the work God does, because God, in his infinite wisdom, grace, and mercy, refuses to force himself upon us.

To read more about spiritual formation, check out the writings of Richard Foster, Scot McKnight, Dallas Willard, and N. T. Wright. These writers have had a tremendous influence on what you've just read.

---

62   Romans 12:1-2

Appendix Four: A Parable For Church Leaders

Then Jesus said, "Whoever has ears to hear, let them hear."
                                                    -Mark 4:9 (NIV)

I remember the first time I joined a health club. It was a "health club" not a "gym," because depending on the water temperature on any given day, it had either a small swimming pool or a large hot tub adjacent to the locker room.

They gave me the MVP treatment the day I signed up. I was single and convinced that the mesmerizingly fit young woman showing me around the facility was going to give me her number at the end of the tour. Instead she asked for mine; my credit card number that is. She said it was the most convenient way to handle monthly billing.

She also told me my initial bill would include a $99 one-time sign-up fee. When I asked what the fee was for, she said it was an administrative fee. Had she not been so beautiful, I might have realized she was charging me a hundred bucks for filling out a form and processing my credit card. Then she quickly added that the sign-up fee also included a training session with one of the club's certified personal trainers. That's when she handed me off to a hulk of a man with muscular earlobes that we'll call Scooby.

Scooby was a nice guy. He asked a few personal questions and we discovered that he had heard of some of the people I knew and I had heard of some of the people he knew, so we were practically best friends. And that's how he treated me, like his best friend. He asked about my fitness goals and nutrition. He showed me some cool exercises and put me through a nice workout. He seemed genuinely interested in helping me get bigger, faster, stronger, and leaner, all at the same time. That $99 sign-up fee was starting to look like a bargain.

After the workout, he showed me the hot tub[63] and told me to take my time. After a nice soak and shower, I walked out of my new health club. I didn't see Sheena, the Amazon Goddess, but I did see Scooby. He told me to take it easy. I told my new best friend that I would. Not only was I a member of a fancy health club, but the friendly staff was there to help me achieve my goals. I looked forward to coming back.

The next day I went in for another workout. When I scanned my card at the counter, the dude sitting there didn't even look up from his muscle magazine. He just waved me through. I looked for Scooby, but didn't see him. Helen of Troy wasn't around either. In fact, none of the helpful and friendly staff who had greeted me the day before was there to receive me. I must have just missed them.

I went back on the third day and was overjoyed to see Miss America working the counter. I scanned my card and she looked up and gave me a polite smile devoid of recognition. Disconcerting, but not surprising. I was single for a reason; it wasn't just my earlobes that were flabby.

---

63   It was a hot water day.

I saw Scooby in the hallway between the cardio and weight rooms. I said "Hey!" and he gave me a perfunctory head nod. He was showing some new guy around. They were acting like best friends. I saw him a few more times over the next month. Eventually I stopped speaking and he stopped nodding. We were no longer friends.

It didn't take me long to get with the program.

I'd walk in, scan my card, ignore the guy behind the counter who was ignoring me, change clothes in the locker room, do 20 minutes of cardio and 20 minutes of weights, soak in the hot tub for 10 minutes or swim 500 laps in the pool,[64] shower, get dressed, and ignore the guy behind the counter as he told the back of my head to have a nice day as I walked out the door.

I worked out there for a couple of years and managed to increase my bench press by five pounds while adding 15 pounds of fat to my already doughy frame.

Everyday I'd show up, workout, and show no progress whatsoever. If anything, I was moving backward. My increase in bench press was more the result of maxing out while the Ice Goddess was walking through the weight room than an increase in actual strength.

During that time, no one from the staff ever said anything to me about my lack of progress. No one ever grabbed me in the weight room and said, "I've been watching you for a month and you're not getting any stronger. Do you want some help?"

The dude at the front desk never said to me as I walked in, "Man, I see you come in every day. You're paying good money to work out here. Why are you getting fatter?"

---

64   My stroke didn't improve but my turns were efficient!

When I took a month off during the summer, no one called to make sure I was okay. They didn't even miss me. The only time I heard anything from the staff was when my credit card expired and they needed me to update my information so they could keep processing my payments. They were running the kind of health club where lack of improvement and increased body fat was nothing to be worried about as long as you kept your credit card up to date.

When I moved, they demanded I show proof that I was leaving the area before they would cancel my contract. My need to keep buying bigger pants was not proof enough that I was no longer a committed customer.

Luckily, I was able to find a gym in my new city that offered a similar arrangement. They took my money and I kept showing up day after day with no discernible improvement. I was happy to have a place to work out and they were happy to scan my credit card. They didn't expect me to get results and I wasn't bothered by their lack of expectations. Going to the gym was part of my routine. Working out everyday and not getting results became the norm for me and just about everyone else on the same treadmill.

"Working out at the gym" is just something middle-class Americans do.

It's a box we're happy to check off for a reasonable monthly fee.

Acknowledgements

Special thanks to:

Mark Riddle for introducing me to CrossFit. Eric Barber for teaching me how to do CrossFit without having my spine shoot out my back and ricochet around the room. Coach Greg Glassman for getting the CrossFit party started. Luke Norsworthy for reading every word I wrote at every stage of composition and offering honest feedback. Donna Urban, Nancy Ulrich, Ron Clarkson, Jason Graves and Jeffrey Keele. They read a preview copy and made several helpful suggestions. Jeremy Mitts and Judy Skelton for the editing expertise. The athletes at Next Generation CrossFit who helped me get off the floor. The gang at the Louis Henna Starbucks in Round Rock, Texas. I wrote 95% of this book while drinking their coffee. My friends who, when I shared with them my thoughts on spiritual fitness, kept saying, "That would make a great book!" Heather, my beautiful wife, for helping with every aspect of this book. She read countless early drafts, helped edit the final version, worked on the cover art, and kept encouraging me to keep going when I was ready to quit. She also sets a great example as a CrossFitting Christ-follower. Caleb and Elijah, my two boys. Their very existence keeps me training for something greater. You, my readers, for reading this far. May you be strong to be useful!

About The Author

Wade is the Senior Minister for the Preston Road Church of Christ. He's a Certified Level One CrossFit Trainer. He loves to cook red meat, listen to audio books, and drink coffee. He's chasing a four-minute Fran and a bodyweight snatch. He lives in Dallas, Texas with his wife, Heather, and two sons, Caleb and Elijah.

You can reach him at wadehodges@gmail.com.

You can find more of his work at www.wadehodges.com.

Made in the USA
San Bernardino, CA
19 November 2013